FUTURE SCOPE

SUCCESS STRATEGIES FOR THE 1990S & BEYOND

JOE CAPPO

Longman Financial Services Publishing
a division of Longman Financial Services Institute, Inc.

While a great deal of care has been taken to provide accurate and current information, the ideas, suggestions, general principles and conclusions presented in this book are subject to local, state and federal laws and regulations, court cases and any revisions of same. The reader is thus urged to consult legal counsel regarding any points of law – this publication should not be used as a substitute for competent legal advice.

Executive Editor: Kathleen A. Welton
Project Editor: Jack L. Kiburz
Interior Design: Sara Shelton

© 1990 by Joe Cappo

Published by Longman Financial Services Publishing,
a division of Longman Financial Services Institute, Inc.

Printed in the United States of America

90 91 92 10 9 8 7 6 5 4 3 2 1

Library of Congress Cataloging-in-Publication Data

Cappo, Joe.
    Futurescope: success strategies for the 1990s and beyond / Joe Cappo.
    p.   cm.
    ISBN 0-88462-919-8
    1. Economic forecasting – United States.   2. United States – Economic conditions – 1981-   3. Social prediction – United States.   4. United States – Social conditions – 1980-   5. Twentieth century – Forecasts.   I. Title.
HC106.8.C365   1990   89-12625
330.973′001′12 – dc20   CIP

CONTENTS

P R E F A C E

This book is for everyone who expects to live through the 1990s. It is a book for forward-thinking people, people who want to be ready for whatever will confront them in the years to come. Despite the title, this isn't a work of science fiction; nor is it an exercise in social futurism. It is meant to be more practical than that.

My premise in devising the scope of this book was simple: We know that the world is filled with change that eventually will affect our lives. So let's put together a book that will outline some of the changes to take place during the last decade of this century. With that knowledge in hand, we can give readers some pointers about managing that change.

The informed person should realize that change does not represent chaos or confusion, but an opportunity. Those prepared for it will benefit from the change. Others may suffer the consequences.

There undoubtedly will be dozens of futuristic studies published in the coming months as we enter the 1990s. This one is different. First off, this is not a study of how the changing environment is going to affect us in the next decade. Just the opposite. It is a look at how changing Americans are going to affect government, businesses, institutions and each other between now and 2000 A.D.

I have limited the scope of this book to Americans because to do otherwise would be unreasonable. A similar study of *all* the world's countries and cultures would take volumes; there are simply too many to consider.

Second, this book is written from the viewpoint of a business journalist. Although it isn't a business book per se, it *is* intended to be a guide for readers who will run businesses, make investments and choose careers over the next decade.

Finally, I hope I have been able to employ solid journalistic techniques in pointing out the most important and relevant trends and describing them in an interesting and entertaining fashion.

We have attempted to make this book more practical by adding a FutureScope Advisory to the end of each chapter. These are intended to point out major changes or trends identified in the chapter as well as give the reader a suggested strategy for dealing with them. Using the shorthand approach also may help readers who may want to refer back to the book as some of the projections and predictions unfold during the next few years.

A Little Warning

In using this book readers should be aware of some basic limitations. Most of my references are based on generalities. The picture of change in America has been painted with very broad brushstrokes. When I write that Americans are more health conscious than ever before, I obviously do not mean that every single one of us has taken up aerobics and is gorging on oat bran. I am trying to track major movements of a significant percentage of the American public — perhaps not even a majority — whose activities will have an impact on jobs, business, government and other institutions during the 1990s. If it is not mentioned throughout this book as examples are given, then I will state right now that there are exceptions to every rule, every trend, movement, fad and fashion enumerated in these pages. For the sake of brevity, many of these exceptions are ignored.

I also should point out that this is basically an anecdotal work, reinforced in appropriate spots by statistics. Many of the conclusions reached are subjective evaluations of the changes taking place. This was never intended to be an academic exercise, research paper or scientific treatise on the subject matter covered here. Indeed, the subject of change in contemporary society and the study of the speculative future are often overlooked or underestimated in college curricula.

Three basic code words are used in this book in forecasting trends: *projections*, *predictions* and *guesses*. There are important distinctions among the three words.

Projections, based on official data and solid research, have roughly a 95% chance of being correct. *Predictions* involve additional interpretation and extrapolation and are less reliable, with an accuracy factor ranging from 75% to 95%. *Guesses* are calculated guesses, not wild stabs. I have resorted to them when trends are new or not definitive; or when good data were not available. I can only hope that 60% to 75% turn out to be accurate.

As I tried to sketch out a profile of American society in 2000, I occasionally looked further down the road to point out significant events that are likely to take place more deeply into the twenty-first century. The further we look into the future, the more chance there is that even our projections will be off the mark.

I am indebted to many different individuals and institutions that contributed to this book, not the least of which is the U.S. government. The Census Bureau, the Bureau of Labor Statistics and dozens of other agencies produce mountains of information every year.

The single most valuable tool for me was the *Statistical Abstract of the United States,* an annual publication I have used for years as a source for newspaper columns and radio commentaries. The *Abstract* is an excellent weapon in repelling uninformed readers and listeners—even government officials and academicians—who speak more from prejudice than from knowledge.

Much of my motivation in attempting this book, in fact, was based on the observation that there is a wealth of statistics, research and other information that never gets back to the public in usable form. (After all, the public is paying for much of it.)

I also must tip my hat to the dozens of other publications, research companies, trade associations, professional organizations, professors, journalists and futurists from whom I borrowed information or ideas. In planning this book we decided not to cite the source of every statistic or piece of data because to do so would affect readability. I take no credit for any research reported in these pages.

My deepest appreciation must also be extended to Kathy Welton, my Longman editor who helped me develop the theme and then coached me in how to write a book—as opposed to the 800-word newspaper column I have been writing for 20 years.

I also am indebted to my industrious researcher, Peter Cunningham, who was often asked to track down some obscure bits of information; my loyal secretary, Mary Hryniszak, who helped me organize this book as she has helped me organize my business life for several years; and my boss, Rance Crain, who has always given me the freedom to expand my horizons.

No one could have received more support and enthusiasm than I did from my family during the year I spent working on this book. My wife, Mary Anne, was a saint for putting up with my many weekends of isolation and the late-night screeching of the computer printer. My daughter, Elizabeth, and son, J. J., were a constant source of inspiration, motivation and encouragement.

I also owe a lot to the guy who invented the computer. I don't know how they wrote books before.

PART 1

AMERICANS IN TRANSITION

CHAPTER 1

The Challenge of Predicting the Future

This is the beginning of the end of the twentieth century. We have ten years to go. One brief decade. The 1990s will flash by even more quickly than the 1980s. Before we know it, we will be perched on the very edge of this century, eagerly waiting to leap into the next. December 31, 1999, will be a tumultuous and emotional day for billions of people. It will mark that special New Year's Eve in which we say good-bye not only to a year, but to a whole century.

The last time we lived through such an experience, William McKinley was president of the United States. Automobiles were rarely seen on city streets. Except for the Wright brothers, no one was even thinking about airplanes. Landing on the moon was something many believed would never happen. And computers . . . well, how could you explain to someone in 1900 what a computer could do?

There has been a tremendous degree of change in the twentieth century. In terms of science and technology, more mind-boggling innovations have altered our lives in the past 90 years than in any other century in the history of mankind. And 10% of the century is still left!

Between now and December 31, 1999, the change will continue, and its pace will not slacken. Indeed, the pace will accelerate as we barge into the twenty-first century. Much of the acceleration in recent years has been generated by the speed of communication and the ease of transportation. From spy satellites to cellular telephones to pocket-size television sets, we are virtually in constant contact with each other. Knowing about events right away enables us to respond more promptly to them. The faster we respond, the faster changes occur.

Technological changes have come in rapid succession over the past four decades, but they are not the only kind of changes taking place; nor are they the most important. Far more significant are changes in world politics and in our physical environment. But more important ultimately is the way human beings are changing.

We can probably assume that the movement in the Soviet Union toward *glasnost* and *perestroika* will have a greater impact on our future than most technological breakthroughs of the next decade. It is certainly far more important than the development of missiles, nuclear weapons and heavy bombers. All of the sophisticated military hardware is meaningless if competing powers don't want to make war with each other.

The computer, arguably the most important technological innovation of the twentieth century, has had a tremendous impact on our economy and our lives. It will certainly become more ubiquitous in the coming years and will help shape the world in the next decade. But the importance of the computer will expand in the decade to come because computer power will be put in the hands of the people. And it will change our lives.

If scientific clues turn out to be true, the greenhouse effect will also alter the way we live. It could create a meteorological chain of events that will have biological, agricultural, medical, commercial, political, diplomatic and psychological implications. It may be the most significant transition to our planet since the melting of the glaciers. The AIDS epidemic, which has altered the lifestyles of millions of people across the world, will continue to make an impact on society in the 1990s. At this writing, there is little hope for a medical solution to AIDS in the near future.

Slow progress has been made on another scourge, cancer, in the past 20 years. Earlier diagnosis and more sophisticated treatment, however, have saved and extended many lives. Because so much research continues on the various forms of cancer, the possibility of breakthroughs in the next decade are very good.

All these monumental transitions are taking place as you read this book. They are among the most influential trends that are shaping the world. But they don't tell the whole story of how or why the world is changing. If we want to delve even more deeply into the causes of change, we must look elsewhere: at *ourselves*.

A Different View of Change

Although this book alludes to some of the massive changes in the world, its primary focus will be on a more modest subject: human beings, specifically American human beings. The basic premise is this: We Americans are changing. We are changing in virtually every way there is to change—our age, our skin color, our family size, our educational level, our taste in products, our work habits, our political inclinations and even our outlook on religion.

More than that, we are saying that people are the most important beings on earth. We are not helpless pawns in the inevitable evolution of society. Except for what insurance companies call acts of God, it is human beings who start wars and negotiate peace, develop technological marvels, prompt companies to market certain products, pollute harbors and feed the hungry.

We are a complex society and to a great degree, especially in this country, can influence our own fate. Most so-called external changes are generated by human beings. Even the greenhouse effect has been blamed on the use of various chemicals and synthetics developed by humans.

That is why we have set out to study how the American personality is changing. Every shift in consumer behavior is magnified and reflected throughout society. These evolutionary trends create some businesses while simultaneously eliminating others. The marketing expert and the astute politician try to keep track of the trends as they develop, because they know there will be an impact on all or part of society.

Look at what has happened to the food industry because of the growing body of knowledge medical researchers have developed about cholesterol. When millions of Americans with high cholesterol levels learned that their conditions could lead to early heart disease, many of them changed their lifestyles and eating habits.

Consumer reaction to the cholesterol danger has sent shock waves through several industries. Per capita consumption of high-cholesterol foods such as red meat, eggs and milk has declined substantially in the past decade. Even though cholesterol concerns have had a negative effect on those who produce and sell high-cholesterol foods, they have had a positive effect on the health care industry. One example is blood testing, which has grown into a major industry in the United States. As we step into the 1990s, Americans are spending nearly $10 billion a year to have their blood tested. This is only one of dozens of consumer trends that are unfolding as we move into the next decade. We are gradually being transformed into different beings, with the end result that in 2000 the profile of the "average American" will be significantly different from that of 1990.

These new Americans will prompt all kinds of changes in the world around us:

- Supermarket operators will change the way they run their stores in order to accommodate shifts in our shopping habits.
- Employers will have to pay higher wages to entry-level employees because fewer of them will be entering the work force in the next decade.
- Politicians will alter their position on government-sponsored child care as the number of working (and voting) mothers increases.
- Marketers will respond to the growing ranks of the elderly by developing products aimed specifically at that age group.
- Government will be forced to restructure our Social Security system when Baby Boomers start reaching retirement age in the early 2000s.
- Corporations will move their operations to distant exurbs of major cities, and even into smaller towns, in response to worker demand for affordable and uncongested living conditions.

These are only a handful of the different reactions our transforming population will evoke from companies, institutions and other individuals. These responses to market changes are necessary for any entity to retain its value. If consumers change, then the public and private enterprises that serve those consumers must change or risk becoming irrelevant.

This has already happened to many businesses that failed to respond properly to changes in the marketplace. Dozens of mid-priced department stores and department store chains refused to recognize the attraction that discount stores would have for shoppers. Consequently, the junkyard of merchandising is filled with the rusting hulks of inflexible retailers who met the same fate as the dinosaurs who failed to respond to change in the environment.

Responding properly to trends and transitions is an essential element of survival. But there is another technique that can provide an even more effective competitive edge: the ability to *anticipate* the change. This isn't an exercise in soothsaying or clairvoyance. There is, after all, a great difference between fortune-telling and forecasting.

The Fine Art of Forecasting

A major component of forecasting is the ability to make accurate projections of current trends. In some cases, this isn't as difficult as it may appear. In dealing with the future age mix of the American population, for example, we can tell with a great deal of certainty that the number of Americans in their 20s will decrease substantially in the 1990s. We are confident about that because the number of teenagers in the country has declined in the 1980s. That is a projection, and an unimpeachable one.

When we predict that this dip in the number of entry-level workers will cause employers to pay more attention to recruiting of young people, that prediction is based on a projection. But the chance of error increases. We are assuming that employers will be smart enough to realize they must take radical steps to combat the labor shortage. There is an outside chance that employers won't have to do anything. But the only way that will happen is if the number of jobs to be filled is reduced substantially, perhaps because of a massive and sustained recession. That, however, is highly unlikely. We think employers will be forced to scramble for workers.

If we went further out on the limb to say that sports car sales will decline in the 1990s because there are fewer people in their 20s, this also would be a prediction based on population projections. That is likely to happen, but such a prediction carries an even greater risk of error. The reason is that sales of various car types are subject to many influences besides age. One is the capricious taste of Americans for various kinds of cars, something no one can gauge with any great degree of reliability. We have made a safer prediction—but still a prediction—in this book: that the shrinking number of potential car buyers in their 20s will lead to a decline in total car sales in the 1990s.

Readers will readily note that one doesn't have to hold a doctorate in future studies to start looking at the future with a more analytical eye. The changes are sometimes obvious, although how to capitalize on them is sometimes not so obvious.

Whether a company is big or small has no bearing on how well it can cope with a changing environment. Earlier in this century we saw thousands of mom-and-pop grocery stores put out of business because supermarkets revolutionized food retailing. Mom-and-pop stores couldn't or didn't respond to the change in the market. But not much later the largest food retailer of all, the Great Atlantic & Pacific Tea Company, fell on hard times and was forced to retrench because it also didn't respond appropriately to the change. Size, then, is not as important as a company's outlook, attitude and ability to adapt.

The Best-Laid Plans . . .

At this point it is important for all budding forecasters to recognize that occasionally happenings are beyond anyone's power to predict. We can't predict whether an earthquake will swallow California, whether Australia will declare war on Austria, whether we will discover life on other planets, whether an eminent scientist will prove that heaven exists. All of these are imponderables that can turn today's predictions into tomorrow's jokes.

Aside from the unforeseeable cataclysms and revolutionary breakthroughs, another situation constantly hinders an unobscured vision of the future: We don't have one-dimensional trends and evolutions all moving together in the same direction toward one inevitable goal. What we have is a mishmash of currents and crosscurrents that sometimes fail to signal where we are headed.

American consumers, for instance, tell supermarket operators that they want to do all of their shopping in one store rather than chase after loss leaders from one store to the next. They apparently want convenient one-stop shopping. At the same time, consumers are demonstrating a distinct tendency to shop in specialty stores rather than in department stores with wide varieties of merchandise. They apparently want retailers who specialize in specific categories.

These trends appear to be contradictory, but both exist and what their coexistence proves is that analyzing American tastes and motives is not as easy as it may appear to a casual observer. We have a deeply ingrained tradition of freedom of choice, and we have exercised that freedom with a vengeance.

In trying to predict the course of future trends, we measure two different kinds of changes taking place among Americans: demographic and psychographic. Demographic changes deal with the vital statistics of our society, such as age, race, marital status, income levels and the like. These can be charted, historical trends can be noted and projections for the next decade can be made. Psychographic changes are not as easy to pin down. They cover the interests, attitudes and psychology of Americans, dealing with topics such as lifestyles, religious preferences, politics, consumer tastes, relationships and other aspects of our society. These obviously are more difficult to measure and to predict, but they are equally important.

Seeking the American Culture

Much has been written in recent years about the globalization of virtually everything. We can't deny that it is happening. We have growing international trade, global telecommunications and worldwide trading of securities. We are doing more international travel. We even have global bankruptcy in the form of massive loan defaults by underdeveloped countries. National Football League games have been played in Europe. American college basketball tournaments have been staged in Japan. That is impressive evidence of the premise of internationalism. And yet, a gulf of difference exists between the average American and the average citizen of any other country.

Is there a distinctly American culture? There is no question about it. Our national traits may not be as old, but they are as distinctive as those of the Italians, the Japanese or the Egyptians. Even though we come from a multitude of backgrounds, an American personality

is emerging from the aggregate of our backgrounds. This American-
ism is felt most vividly by immigrants who live here for a few years,
then return to their homelands to find that they don't fit in as tightly
as they once did.

This doesn't mean that Americans speak with one voice. The United
States is still very much a pluralistic society, probably more diverse
than any other country. Much of our personality is derived from
that diversity.

As we mature as a nation we tend to grow more alike, the same
way a husband and wife are said to start looking, sounding and act-
ing alike the longer they live together. But all of this is tempered
by the constant flow of immigrants to our shores. New ingredients
are always being added to the stew of American society, changing
its color, taste and texture. That might account for the admittedly
intuitive observation that we tend to change more than other cultures.
We have more influences being exerted upon us than any other country. We have a greater access to communications and a greater array
of products, services and options available to us. But most of all,
we seem to be more amenable to change. There are no charts, tables
or graphs to prove this contention. But one would be hard-pressed
to find any other society that is as adaptable to change as we are in
the United States.

How to Use This Book

The purpose of this book is to open the reader's mind to the possi-
bilities and pitfalls of the next decade. Business experts have said,
with good reason, that American corporations have developed too
much of a short-term mentality. That is, companies will sacrifice their
future for the sake of producing a good quarterly report. This concentration on short-term results prompted many American industrial
companies to curtail their investment in research and development
during the 1970s. They were more intent on bringing in profits because that would buoy up the price of their stock, and that's what
the shareholders wanted; or at least that's what the shareholders
thought they wanted.

As a result, many American industries lost their competitive edge
in the marketplace. They were overtaken by foreign companies

investing in new plants and updating equipment while the American companies were squeezing more dollars onto the bottom line. Any company that makes its decisions with an eye toward the next decade should be able to avoid these disastrous consequences. Digesting the principles in this book represents only one step that should be taken by enlightened companies. We are, after all, dealing with only one aspect of the future: how the American consumer will change.

A multitude of other future topics will have to be studied. Companies must also anticipate changes in technology, international competition, trade alliances, foreign affairs, public policy, federal and local legislation and every other influence on their businesses.

There is one real way for companies to deal with the future: put somebody in charge of it. With all the functions management performs, none would be more crucial than plotting future trends and determining how they will affect the company. Corporations with executives in charge of public affairs and consumer affairs should be able to afford an executive in charge of future affairs.

For those companies that market to the American public, the following chapters will serve as an informal guide for the next ten years. By recognizing the changes taking place among Americans, marketers should be able to anticipate future demand for specific items and identify market niches that are developing for new products and services. Many major companies are already doing this, of course, but many others are not; and most medium-size and smaller companies seldom plan more than one or two years into the future. Strategic planning became one of the hot areas of the 1980s, although it was greatly overshadowed by the storm of mergers and acquisitions, which typifies the short-term mentality in action. We don't have to develop any new products, the acquisition-minded megacorporations say. All we have to do, they maintain, is acquire a company that has some good products to sell. As a result, capital that could have gone into building plants and equipment, into research on new technologies or into introduction of new products, goes instead into buying the stock of other companies. This is usually accompanied by the handsome compensation of management. Many people, it seems, don't see the distinction between building a business and buying one that someone else has built. Perhaps building a business takes too long.

For Entrepreneurs and Individuals

Another category of businesspeople who must adopt the principles of *FutureScope* are the millions of entrepreneurs and small-business operators who can't afford to hire a staff of strategic planners, marketing executives and new product innovators. They obviously aren't big enough to have a vice president in charge of future affairs, but someone, perhaps even the owner, should be assigned to do some future exploration. These enterprises can benefit from anticipating the future more than the big guys can because they are more flexible and are not pressured by shareholder demand for profitable quarterly reports. Being flexible is meaningless, though, if a company has no plan for tracking change in the marketplace and doing something about it.

Statistics show that a preponderance of new businesses fail within the first few years. Maybe not looking far enough into the future is one reason for this. Even for those who do not run businesses, there is good reason for scoping the future. Many individuals are trying to determine what occupations will yield the greatest success for them in the next decade. There is an ebb and flow to the job market that we have tried to capture in these pages—not that this is a career guide or aptitude test. Look at *FutureScope* as a book-length brainstorming session.

We have tried to enumerate hundreds of trends and ideas for the 1990s, all intended to help readers evaluate various courses of action for the 1990s. Strategic planning, after all, should not be reserved exclusively for corporations. Each individual should develop his or her own personal strategic plan for the future. The best way to start is by looking down the long road of the 1990s and anticipating the dips and curves in that road. Each of us—individual, enterprise or institution—will confront a myriad of changes in the decade ahead. The difference between survival and failure will depend on how astutely we anticipate these changes and how effectively we respond to them. By 2000 A.D., we will know how well we did.

FUTURE SCOPE

*A*DVISORY

Trends

- Everything is in a state of flux. Nothing ever stays the same.

- Americans are changing constantly, both demographically and psychographically. This change in our nature will force institutions and enterprises to adapt to us.

- Companies that fail to respond to changes in the marketplace are in danger of losing market share or even going out of business.

- Choosing the appropriate response isn't easy because so many changes are occurring at the same time, often working against each other.

Strategies

- It is imperative that every corporation, institution and individual plan for the future.

- Analyze current trends and use the results to anticipate changes that are likely to occur. Plan to respond as early as possible, while monitoring any shift in key trends.

- Corporations should consider appointing an executive to be in charge of studying future affairs.

CHAPTER 2

The Population Machine Runs Out of Steam

Of all the transitions occurring simultaneously in our society, none of them is more important than the shifts in our population age mix. Most of the transitions identified in this book will affect millions of us by the year 2000. But the restructuring of our population will leave none of us untouched by its influence.

If you study what is happening to the U.S. population, two trends stick out like sore thumbs. The first is that our population has virtually stopped growing. The second is that we are older than we ever have been before. These two factors are linked together in several ways, but because they are both important to what happens in the next decade, we'll treat them separately. Each of them will be exerting different influences on the world around us.

The United States enters 1990 with about 250 million in population, an increase of about 10% during the 1980s. In the 1970s, population increased by 11%; in the 1960s, by 13%; and in the 1950s, by 19%. There is no question that our growth is ebbing. Our population slowdown can be attributed to several factors, but the most obvious is that American women are not having as many children as they did in previous generations. The fertility rate is not merely declining; it has plummeted dramatically in the past 30 years.

Demographers estimate that in the nineteenth century the average American woman had six to seven children during her childbearing years. With only one exception, this fertility rate has declined steadily since that time. The exception occurred in the 1950s and 1960s, during that period best known as the Baby Boom. Those Americans born between 1946 and 1964 are known as Baby Boomers, an expression that will be used often throughout this book. Baby Boomers are not to be confused with the age cohort known as Baby Busters, those born between 1965 and 1976, the years in which the birthrate resumed its long-term slide. As you will read in the pages ahead, Boomers and Busters will both have a tremendous impact on our society in the decade to come.

Here is a statistical look at how our birthrate has shifted since World War II. In 1950, the average woman gave birth to 3.0 children, which marked the first uptick in the fertility rate since the early part of the twentieth century. This was influenced heavily by returning veterans who had delayed getting married or having children during the war.

By 1957, which was the hottest postwar year for baby production, the fertility rate had climbed to 3.7. Since then, however, the fertility rate continued its long-term decline, dropping in 1976 to 1.7, the lowest level ever recorded in history. The rate hovered around 1.8 over the next decade before edging up slightly to 1.9 in 1988. U.S. Census Bureau specialists say that this does not represent the beginning of a long-term rise but probably a result of career women who put off having children until they got into their 30s.

Unless there is a significant upswing in the fertility rate, the U.S. population will stop growing sometime in the twenty-first century. There is no telling exactly when it will happen, which is why the U.S. Census Bureau makes a range of three projections. The "middle series" projection puts the date of zero population growth (ZPG) at 2038. Based on the most recent projections, our population will hit 302 million in that year and then is expected to start a slow decline. It should level off later on in the twenty-first century, but statisticians warn that the degree of uncertainty increases as the projections go further into the future.

Here is our projection of how the U.S. population will peak in the next 60 years:

Year	Population	% Increase
1990	249,891	10.3
2000	267,747	7.1
2010	281,669	5.2
2020	291,809	3.6
2030	298,228	2.2
2040	302,104	1.3
2050	301,500	−0.2

These projections account for immigration at current levels. If the immigration flow changes substantially, it may alter the projections.

If you believe the "lowest series" projection, ZPG can occur as early as 2015, only 25 years out from 1990. The "highest series" projection, meanwhile, indicates that the U.S. population will keep rising indefinitely. This projection is not to be taken seriously. In recent years most of the adjustments made to projections have pushed the population curve downward.

Conventional theory among demographers is that 2.1 births per woman is our "replacement rate," the level of births we would need over the long haul to keep our population at a constant level. We have already dropped below the 2.1 threshold, and we are probably going to stay there for the foreseeable future. This trend troubles some demographers, including Ben Wattenberg, author of *The Birth Dearth.* He believes that the United States and other Western democracies with low fertility rates will be passed up in population by Third World countries that are growing rapidly. As the populations of other countries grow, he maintains, America's influence on the world will be reduced.

Even if his contention has some validity to it, there will be no impact on our worldwide standing in the next decade, and probably not even in the next century. Our influence on the world is more likely to decline because of faulty economic policies and inept diplomacy rather than a declining population. But population politics will attract more attention as we approach ZPG. It might well develop into one of the key issues of the 1990s, with conservatives being most fearful that our lagging population will tend to erode our world influence.

One might also ask why our population continues to grow, even though the fertility rate has been so low. It is because those millions of Baby Boomers are in the midst of their childbearing years. More women than ever are able to have babies, even though they are not having as many children as their mothers did. And so, as we steadily head toward ZPG there has been a modest blip in the number of young children, offspring of the Boomers. This bubble is usually called the Echo Boom or Baby Boomlet, and it has already run its course.

The Art of Controlling Births

There are several obvious reasons why the fertility rate has declined to such a low level. Perhaps the most important is that the Baby Boomers simply don't want as many children as the previous generation did. They are also equipped with something that their parents didn't have, a wide variety of effective birth control measures—and they are using them. An estimated 93% of women age 18 to 44 who are exposed to the risk of pregnancy use some form of birth control, with the pill being the most common. (Women who are not exposed to the risk of pregnancy include those who (1) are pregnant or trying to become pregnant; (2) are infertile; (3) have been sterilized; or (4) abstain from sexual activity.) This leaves only a small percentage of women of childbearing age who are not using any birth control measures. The major difference over the past 40 years is that couples have far more control over determining when they will have children. That was far more difficult before the development of oral contraceptives, intrauterine devices and other methods of birth control.

But there are other reasons contributing to the slide. Young Americans are getting married at more advanced ages than they were a few years back, and consequently they are starting families later in life. Thus they have fewer family-forming years. Back in 1890, the first time it was measured, the median marriage age for women in the United States was 22 years, and for men 26.1. But between 1947 and 1962, the median marriage age dropped to a low of 20.3 for women and 22.6 for men. This has since rebounded to a record high in 1988 of 23.6 for women and 25.9 for men. While the difference in years seems minor, by demographic standards it represents a substantial aging of those getting married for the first time. As far as the next decade is concerned, we believe that the median marriage age for both men and women will tend to move upward at a slow but steady rate.

There is a multitude of reasons for later marriages, but the one we lean to, partly with tongue in cheek, is that young singles in this country are having too much fun to get married. If all of the couples who are living together got married immediately, it would shoot the marriage statistics off the charts. The explosion in the number of women going into professions, of course, is probably exerting an even more important influence on the marriage age.

Another reason for the lower birthrate is that a growing proportion of Americans will never get married and start a family. This trend has just recently attracted the attention of the Census Bureau, and there is a controversy over methods of projecting these figures into the future. Some demographers believe that the percentage of never-marrieds in our population might grow to be two or three times as high as it was in the 1950s. The most dramatic statistics come in a comparison of men and women in the 25–34 age group. The percentage of those never married in that age group was more than twice as high in 1987 than it was in 1970. If this trend continues to grow as it has in the past 20 years, it may signal an even sooner arrival at ZPG.

Aside from birthrates, our population growth is also affected by immigration. The number of immigrants to the United States has increased in the past few years, buoying up our population even though our fertility rate is below the replacement rate. Currently, immigration accounts for nearly one-third of our population growth. By the first decade of the twenty-first century, probably all of our growth will come from immigration. Even so, immigration can't compensate for a fertility rate that is half what it was 30 years ago. The only way that immigration will push ZPG to a later date is if new immigrants have a significantly higher fertility rate that might affect the national rate.

Hispanics make up the biggest proportion of U.S. immigrants, and their fertility rate is about twice as high as the rate for native Americans. Realistically, however, the number of immigrants coming into the country would have to swell substantially to push our fertility rate above the replacement level.

Remember that the number of immigrants and the higher immigrant birthrate is factored into the national totals that we have been discussing. Without them, we would have reached ZPG years ago.

Overestimating the Boom

Tracking population levels has become more important in recent years because it should help us avoid some of the problems that sprang up during the post–Baby Boom years. When the population explosion erupted after World War II, governments and businesses apparently believed it would never stop. They failed to realize that the Baby Boom was an unusual blip on the nation's predominantly flat growth curve. One demographer described the Baby Boom as being like a python that swallowed a whole piglet: You can see the bulge as it travels down the snake's digestive system.

There was a simple explanation for the boom. We had more births during the 1946–64 period because World War II had delayed family plans for millions of Americans. The rush of marriages in 1946—a remarkable 42% over 1945—was an anomaly, not a new trend. Likewise, the burst of births that started in 1946 was also a temporary condition; unfortunately, many institutions failed to see this. They surmised—incorrectly—that our birthrate was returning to its pre-depression level. Nowhere was this more evident than in the educational world.

Faced with a bulging preschool population in the early 1950s, boards of education across the country went on a school-building binge. This continued into the 1960s, and into the 1970s even though the number of births had already started to fall. By the early 1980s, school districts, especially in large cities and old established suburbs, were forced to close schools because the supply of children was drying up. In some suburbs, schools built as recently as 15 years earlier had to be shuttered, and teachers recruited as recently as the preceding year had to be laid off. Even as we enter 1990 some cities and towns are still dotted with school buildings no longer used for educational purposes. In some districts, taxpayers are still paying for buildings that sit there unused.

The birthrate slowed so rapidly that between 1980 and 1987, the number of teenagers in the country had declined by 10%. (In some areas, the number of teenagers declined by 20% or more.) By then, college administrators realized that they too were facing the same kind of trouble. Basic common sense told them that the fewer high school students there were, then the fewer college applicants there would be four years down the road. The dip in college enrollments began in the late 1980s but is expected to slip even more as we proceed through the next decade. Some estimates indicate that as many as 100 to 250 colleges will have to close their doors or merge with other institutions because of declining enrollments.

What might alter that projection, though, is something that the statisticians couldn't count on. The percentage of high school students applying for college increased significantly. Another factor boosting enrollment was the increased number of adults who decided to go to college after working for a few years or having a family. As a result, college enrollment declined only about 2% throughout the 1980s, although it is certain to dip even more in the early 1990s. The shortage of recruits has led to the creation of a new mini-industry, college marketing, which includes a growing number of firms and consultants. Some college administrators even feel that the impending shortage of students has forced institutions to reevaluate themselves and upgrade their educational "product." (At last word, though, the crisis hadn't caused any colleges or universities to lower their tuition rates.)

The important aspect of this dip in the number of young people, the Baby Busters, is that it will be with us through their lifetimes, just as the Baby Boom will be. If we had 10% fewer teenagers in the 1980s, then we will have 10% fewer people in their 20s during the 1990s, 10% fewer people in their 30s during the first decade of the twenty-first century, and so on.

And we should be sure to give a bit of advice to all the boards of education that have some empty buildings on their hands: Don't sell them. You will need some space for the Echo Boomers who are already into the schools. The only point to remember is that they won't have the same impact that the Boomers did 35 years ago.

The Coming Labor Shortage

What this signals for the years ahead is an immediate impact on businesses, especially those who hire a lot of entry-level people. There simply will be fewer of them to go around in the coming decade. By 1995, the number of teenage workers looking for jobs is estimated to be about 20% lower than it was in 1975. Many demographers are predicting a substantial shortage of new workers for virtually every business and industry. This will result in more intense recruiting of young workers by corporations.

The labor shortage also will lead to disproportionately higher starting salaries for newcomers. The danger in this is that it might create an age/wage crisis in which entry-level workers are paid more than veteran workers. But few employees will be victimized. The 1990s will develop into an unprecedented workers' market, which will put tremendous pressure on all kinds of businesses. The only industries not affected will be those that are shrinking, primarily blue-collar manufacturing operations. This sector of the economy will produce very few new jobs in the next ten years.

The imbalance in the number of jobs created and the lagging supply of labor has already contributed to a significantly lower unemployment rate in the late 1980s, the lowest in nearly 20 years. The ratios indicate very strongly that this imbalance will continue at least until the late 1990s, when the Echo Boomers start coming into the job market. The competition for college graduates will heat up considerably in the next couple of years. The number of college graduates will start to decline while corporations are creating a greater number of jobs that require a college education. Chapter 9 will take a closer look at specific occupations and professions that will grow most rapidly in the next decade.

Companies that have to hire a lot of college graduates will start their recruiting earlier than they did in previous years. They also will try to hire college students as interns during school breaks as a means of recruiting. When the student finally graduates, he or she will be more likely to join the same company. We predict that employers will also start offering scholarships to students, paying their way through graduate school, for example, if the student agrees to join the company at a set salary level upon completion of his or her degree work. Whatever the strategy used, the shortage of young people entering the job market will probably be the single biggest challenge for American industry in the 1990s.

Even hurt more than private industry will be the armed forces, whose total recruitment effort is aimed at 18- to 21-year-olds. In order to attract recruits, the services will have to compete with industry, offering higher pay, more liberal college benefits and better working conditions. The armed forces already spend hundreds of millions of dollars in media advertising to attract young people, and this stands to increase in the next few years. If the armed forces are not able to maintain their current level of recruits, we might see increased pressure on Congress to reimpose the military draft.

One trend that will help the military, as well as private industry, is the number of women entering the work force. There definitely will be more women in uniform in all of the services in the 1990s. Of course, the best way for the United States to solve the military problem would be to press forward with peace talks with the Soviet Union. The chances of that happening are brighter now than they have been at any time since the end of World War II.

Another government manuever to alleviate the impending labor shortage has already started. The United States is asking its allies to take on increased defense responsibilities. Let *them* scramble to get young people into the military.

Some Answers to the Problem

A higher percentage of women, including mothers, is entering the work force, which should help relieve some of the pressure on the job market. The labor shortage might turn out to be the most effective way of achieving job equality for women. Some fields and companies that previously ignored women might be putting out the welcome mat for them. But even here, don't look for any magical solutions. The number and percentage of women going to work has increased for years but has started to slow down in the past couple of years. Labor experts expect that the number may stabilize in the next few years.

Immigrants also may pick up some of the slack but only in areas where there is demand for unskilled labor. Most of the jobs being created are in service and technical areas, which necessitate specific training or at least a working knowledge of English. Most of the immigrants are coming in from Mexico and other Hispanic countries and don't have the level of education to meet the demand for higher paying jobs.

Another bit of help might come from the more effective use of automation and robotics by American industry, reducing the need for blue-collar workers. This trend, in fact, started years ago and has contributed to a decline of thousands of manufacturing jobs. That, coupled with the competition for manufacturing from Third World countries, created a disaster among the labor forces in some industries. In the coming decade, though, any labor economies achieved through technology will be welcomed as a means of combating the shortage. But increased use of automation creates a different set of needs. The manufacturing worker of tomorrow will have to be better educated than the factory worker of yesteryear. He or she will need sufficient technical skills to operate a computer, a robot or some other sophisticated machinery or controls.

Most labor experts looking into the future predict that manufacturing will not be as important to our economy as it has been for the past century. It will continue to produce revenues that contribute to our gross national product, but it will not create the jobs that it did in the early part of the twentieth century. Virtually every study conducted indicates that the bulk of our growth will come in white-collar service jobs, as well as in professional, technical and managerial positions. These kinds of jobs cannot be eliminated or consolidated by technology as readily as manufacturing jobs are.

The Challenge to Education

The need for more highly skilled and better educated workers is part of the reason that the nation's public education system has come under such intense scrutiny. Many of the systems, especially those in big cities, have been criticized for producing high school graduates who can't even read at an eighth-grade level. The mission of the public school systems supposedly is to provide students with the academic background to get into college or with marketable skills to enter the job market. But the primary challenge of some school systems has turned out to be something even more basic than that; they have to discourage students from dropping out, which in some school districts accounts for more than half of those who start as freshmen. The education crisis will lead to a greater involvement on the part of business in the educational system in the next decade. In

Chicago, for example, a group of corporations has opened its own school on the city's depressed West Side and intends to run it with private contributions.

Over the past 30 years, many American companies have escaped paying high salaries by building manufacturing plants in foreign countries and taking advantage of cheap labor. That opportunity won't be available as a means of fighting the labor shortage because most of the jobs will be service-related and thereby unexportable. The job pressure in the 1990s will be concentrated in such fields as banking, insurance, sales and retailing. There will even be a shortage of teachers because the Echo Boomers will be boosting the demand for education through the year 2000. By then, the number of young people coming out of high schools and colleges will be on the upswing, and the challenge for American industry will be to create enough jobs for all. As the Echo Boomers start coming out of school in the late 1990s, we will shift in a relatively short time from a worker shortage to a worker surplus. That increase, however, will be only a shadow—or an echo—of the Baby Boom. Until then, most employers will have to forget the good old days of the 1980s, when there was an abundance of workers from which to choose.

Facing a No-Growth Market

There is an even more ominous reality facing American industry as we move into the next decade. The slowing of our population growth means that companies will not enjoy the automatic increases in demand that are the by-product of a rapidly growing population. The greatest impact will be felt by consumer products marketers, especially those that turn out parity goods or commodity products such as soap, toothpaste, underwear, and such. When we finally do reach ZPG, these companies will face a supreme marketing challenge. If they want to boost the sales of any product, the only way they can do so will be by taking market share away from competitors. This will not be a new battle in most competitive areas. Consumer products companies have been slugging it out for years, but with a static market the rules are a little different. If you lose market share, your sales go down. Thus the whole marketing process will become more expensive for companies in highly competitive fields.

But we won't have to wait until the middle of the next century for industry to feel the chill of these shifting population patterns. It's going to start for some industries in the next couple of years. A prime example will be the automotive business. A smaller flow of teenagers and college graduates entering the work force also means there will be fewer young people to buy all those sports cars Detroit is turning out. We predict that auto sales will slide considerably over the next six to eight years. The sales decline might well match the projected dip of 10% among young Americans, the prime age cohort at which all the glitzy television commercials are aimed.

Other products aimed largely at a teenage and young adult market will also have fewer potential consumers. An area almost certain to suffer from the dip in young adult consumers is the apartment rental market. Rentals have soared over the years because of the rapid growth in households, many of which were young singles moving out on their own; they were virtually all renters rather than owners. In the 1970s, new households were formed at the rate of about 1.7 million a year. In the 1990s, household growth will slow to less than one million a year. We predict that this will create an unprecedented surplus of rental units on the market.

Unlike consumer products marketers, landlords can't slow down the manufacture of their "product" or reduce their "inventory." One way out of the oncoming crunch may lie in the conversion of rental apartments into condominiums. The prime market for these units would be the growing number of empty nesters—senior Baby Boomers—who want to move out of their homes into smaller dwelling units now that their kids have gone off to college.

Many other industries—ranging from beer to blue jeans—will have to be wary of the 1990s if they depend on young people as their primary markets. Some companies have already made provisions and will be ready for the coming slowdown. They will diversify, change their markets or do whatever it takes to survive the next decade. Other companies will go into the next decade as if everything will be the same as the last decade. These will simply die.

FUTURE SCOPE

—————— ADVISORY ——————

Trends

- U.S. population growth is slowing down as birthrate declines.

- Americans stay single longer, have children later in life and form smaller families.

- The percentage of persons who never marry will double or triple in the 1990s.

- The number of people in their 20s will decline in the 1990s, creating a shortage of college students, prospective entry-level workers and armed forces recruits.

- Slower population growth signals slower growth in demand for all consumer products. Car sales and rental apartments will be hard hit.

- The quality of the public education system continues to decline.

Strategies

- Businesses that hire entry-level people should identify prospects earlier. Interview them a year or more before graduation, offer internships and offer to pay all or part of their tuition.

- Employers should court growing sectors of the work force: women, minorities and older citizens.

- Companies must solidify market share, especially if products are aimed at a no-growth youth market; direct products and services toward a growing middle-age market.

- Prepare for a jump in the number of young adults in the late 1990s, when the Echo Boomers come of age.

CHAPTER 3

Planning for an Older America

A seemingly routine announcement was made by the U.S. Census Bureau a couple of years back. The announcement stated that the leading edge of an American age cohort we know as Baby Boomers had reached age 40 on July 1, 1987. The announcement generated no screaming headlines, was all but ignored by network newscasts, and failed to make the covers of newsweeklies. And yet, the event on which that announcement was based will have a profound impact on all of us, our children and our grandchildren for the next 50 years and beyond.

What this ordinary snippet of information from the census people signifies is that we are growing older. It is no surprise, of course, that each of us is growing older individually. Our bodies remind us of that process every day. But the more important truth is that we are growing older as a nation. Throughout most of our history, the median age of all Americans—the age at which half of us are older and half of us are younger—hovered in the 20s. (It was in the middle teens back in the nineteenth century.) The median popped up to 30 in 1950 because so few babies were born during the war years. The Baby Boom, however, pushed the median age down to 28.1 by 1970.

Those old enough to remember the 1960s may recall that this country was heavily influenced by the youth movement. "Don't trust anyone over 30" was the slogan of that generation. Young people were wielding political and economic power. In college towns, student activists were elected to city councils and even to the post of mayor. Manufacturers hit the market with a tide of items aimed at the young. The era marked a period of great growth for Levi Strauss, the maker of blue jeans.

The late 1960s and early 1970s will be remembered because the period probably produced the greatest gulf in values and attitudes between the young and the old that the United States has ever seen. The Vietnam War had a lot to do with it, of course. In countless cities across the country thousands of young people took to the streets to protest the war. They burned their draft registration cards, broke into draft board offices and destroyed records, and conducted sit-ins at campus buildings. There also were other causes being pressed primarily by the young: civil rights, equal rights for women, freedom of expression, and concern for the poor and oppressed. The young median age we had at the time didn't cause the generation gap, but since half of our population was under 28 it meant that the older generation's influence was ebbing. It was time for the young to make things happen.

As we struggled through the 1970s, however, the fervor of the youth movement died down. Our pulling out of Vietnam eliminated the most obvious cause of the bitter division between young and old. Something else was also happening. The hordes of young activists were being followed by a much smaller cohort of youngsters.

By 1980, the nation's median age hit 30 again, and by 1982 it hit 30.6, the oldest median age ever recorded up until that time. But the aging process didn't stop there. Our national median age has since gone beyond that number and is headed for even higher record levels in the years to come. The median age in 1990 will be 33. By 2000, we will surpass 36; by 2010, we will be nearly 39, and we will move on up into the 40s within the first three decades of the twenty-first century.

Here is a look at how the various age cohorts have shifted over the years, including the middle series projection to 2000:

	1960	1970	1980	1990	2000	% change 1960–2000
		(In thousands)				
Under 5	20,341	17,166	16,458	18,408	16,898	−17
5–17	44,184	52,596	47,237	45,630	48,815	+10
18–34	39,047	50,034	67,976	70,065	62,380	+60
35–54	44,799	46,466	48,622	63,384	81,134	+81
55–74	26,678	31,175	37,415	39,737	42,401	+59
75 and over	5,622	7,614	10,051	13,187	16,639	+196
Total	180,671	205,051	227,759	250,411	268,267	+48

As the table clearly shows, the population of those 35 and over is growing far more rapidly than the under-35 cohort. Between 1980 and 2000, the number of those under 35 will actually decline from 131,671,000 to 128,093,000. At the same time, the number of those 35 and older will grow from 96,088,000 to 140,174,000. The reason that the 55 to 74 age group is smaller than the others is because it represents those born between 1926 and 1945, the low birth era dominated by the Great Depression and World War II.

One thing the table does not show is that the oldest of our senior citizens will increase in age at an even faster pace than the other cohorts. Those aged 85 and older will double between 1980 and 2000, from 2.5 million to 5.0 million. Even more dramatic will be the rise in those who are 100 years of age or older. Their numbers will more than triple, growing from 30,000 in 1980 to 108,000 in 2000.

Facing the Retirement Crisis

These shifts in our age mix will affect many different aspects of society, business and politics. Perhaps the most profound of those changes will be in the ratio of the working-age population to those of retirement age. Back in 1980, there were approximately 5.5 people of working age for every person of retirement age. This will decline modestly by 2000, to 4.7, but will drop sharply to 2.7 in 2030.

The knowledge that the nation is growing older isn't news to most informed citizens who have read numerous stories about the graying of America. Some readers may have thought that although the stories were interesting there was no sense of urgency, no general feeling among the populace that we should examine this trend closely and see whether we could do something to prepare for it. In other words, it hasn't reached a crisis level yet, so let's not worry about it. Will it ever reach a crisis level? No doubt about it. That point won't be reached during the ten-year span that we are concentrating on. But it certainly will occur by 2012. If you wonder why that year is critical I suggest you go back and reread the first paragraph of this chapter. We mentioned then that the first of the Baby Boomers hit 40 years of age in 1987. This means that the first of the Boomers will hit 65 in 2012 and be eligible for retirement benefits. The sheer size of the Boomer age group will send the Social Security formula spinning, unless changes are made in the system between now and then.

These figures show why some forward-looking legislators are issuing warning signals about our current Social Security structure. While most of those who retire and collect Social Security have made the appropriate payments into the system, they are receiving far more in benefits than they ever paid in, even when you add in the interest from their contributions. This means, in effect, that those currently working and paying their Social Security contributions are providing the funds for today's retirees. Another vivid example of how Social Security has increased over the years can be seen when we compare our payments with individual income tax payments. In 1970 Americans paid twice as much in individual income taxes as they did in Social Security contributions.

By the late 1980s, however, income tax payments were only 20% higher. We predict that by the mid-1990s, the Social Security tax paid by employers and employees will be larger than the income tax. It is true that the Social Security formula appears to be working now. Indeed, the system is experiencing a modest surplus every year, which was intended to cushion us against the coming age boom. But by the early years of the twenty-first century, the surplus will be wiped out. And by 2030, the burden on each worker of supporting retirees will more than double. Unless the Social Security structure or benefits change, the next generation of workers will be paying in at least twice the share that goes into the system now.

Another trend also must be factored into the Social Security equation: Americans are living longer. An American born in 1920, for instance, could expect to live 54.1 years. But those Baby Boomers born in 1950 can expect to live 68.2 years, nearly 14 years longer than their parents. And this trend of an expanded lifetime for the average American has continued. Life expectancy for babies born in 1986 is 74.9 years. And those who hit 65 in that year can expect to live another 17 years on the average. By 2000, life expectancy is projected to reach 76.7 years.

There are skeptics, even renowned demographers, who have contended that we aren't living that much longer. They state—and accurately so—that the primary reason life expectancy has expanded is because of improvements in the infant mortality rate. One wrote recently that life expectancy for those age 65 has increased by "only" five years since the beginning of the twentieth century. "Only" five years? If life expectancy for 65-year-olds moved from ten years to 15 years, it represents a 50% increase. That is a substantial shift in expectancy.

What this demographer did was to overlook how important those additional five years are, not only to the person who is going to live them but to the retirement system that is going to support them. As we stated earlier, it isn't a crisis yet. But since our mission is to alert readers to future problems and opportunities, we must reiterate that our increased life span, when compounded by the bubble of Boomers growing older, will demand radical action in the early part of the twenty-first century.

The aging of the population is already creating problems for some corporate pension funds, many of which were established under actuarial tables that assumed much shorter life expectancy. Employers will have to beef up the funds in order to fulfill their obligation to retirees. The problem of unfunded liabilities by many pension funds first came to our attention in the early 1980s and will probably remain a major concern throughout the next decade and beyond. Another related phenomenon will start to occur among older corporations that will find their annual pension payments to retirees will surpass their annual payroll to workers. This trend will continue to expand as work forces shrink, especially among the nation's largest corporations.

Living Longer, Retiring Younger

In considering the shifts in age mix, the projected shortage of labor and the increased longevity of the average American, one might assume that older workers would stay in their jobs longer and delay their retirements. That trend, if broad enough, could help alleviate the coming Social Security crunch. The conventional retirement age of 65 was established by Social Security in the 1930s, when average life expectancy was 60 years. Now that average life expectancy has hit 75 years and is well on its way to reaching 80 years, it would have been fairly reasonable to assume that the retirement age should also be advancing. After all, these over-65 citizens are more active and in better health than any previous generation, and they have more years to live. Unfortunately, all of those factors are having no impact on retirement age. Americans aren't working longer at all. In fact, they are retiring at an earlier age than ever before.

A survey by the Hoover Institution at Stanford University indicates that 87% of male workers retire *before* they reach 65. The most common retirement age among men is 62, but the average is 61, lowered mainly by the impact of those who are retiring as early as age 55. The major component of the latter group consists of those retiring from military service or from federal, state or local government jobs. For some reason it has become traditional for public employees to retire at far earlier ages than private employees. Do you think it is because they work harder? Whatever the reason, there is a substantial number of relatively young persons who have opted to leave the work force. One study pointed out that in 1970, 16% of 60-year-old men were out of the labor force. This had shot up to 29% by 1989. Figures for working women are more difficult to pin down for a variety of reasons, but studies indicate that they generally are lengthening their work lives while men are shortening theirs.

Back in the 1960s and 1970s, poor health was cited most often as the reason for retirement. In effect, senior workers weren't able to keep up with the requirements of their jobs. But as we moved into the 1980s, retirement became more arbitrary for many senior workers who were perfectly capable of continuing on. They had the choice of retiring or staying on the job, and most chose to kiss their jobs goodbye. They were more capable of doing this than any earlier generation. Because of private pension plans and more astute investing, older workers were in more secure financial positions than their predecessors. Prospective retirees still ask themselves whether they can afford to retire, but when they consider the income from Social Security added to their private pensions, the answer is usually yes. But even more important than financial independence, researchers noted that attitudes had changed among American workers. Retirement was no longer a luxury for those lucky to live long enough. Retirement had evolved into an earned right for every individual.

With the combination of a growing worker shortage and increasing retirement burden, there is no question that American industry faces a major challenge in the next decade. In the future, the most effective solution to both of these problems will be to keep older workers on the payroll beyond traditional retirement age. This is a remarkable turnaround from only a dozen or so years ago when some companies, eager to take on younger workers at lower pay scales, were introducing schemes to induce employees to retire early. With a scarcity of younger workers, however, the veterans are looking more attractive to employers.

Companies will likely offer continuation of benefits, such as health and dental care, life insurance, flexible work hours, extended vacations and other features that might entice older workers to stay at their jobs for a few additional years. It also might take money, in the form of salary, bonus and incentives to attract the attention of seniors. American employers also might consider the part-time pension program that the Swedish government has instituted. The normal retirement age in Sweden is 65. When they hit 60, though, workers are given the opportunity to take part-time retirement for the next ten years. They reduce the number of hours they work, with their income consisting of part pay and part pension. This keeps the more experienced and more productive workers on the job until they are 70.

The Age of Opportunity

The aging of our population doesn't present only problems and challenges. It also offers opportunities to companies and individuals. The aging boom can lead to profitable industries and growing occupations. Some of these opportunities are fairly obvious. For example, if the number of Americans 85 and older will double between 1980 and 2000, it stands to reason that the demand for retirement home space will double. But that is only a mathematical ratio. What must be added to the mix is that older persons are more likely to live on their own than they did in previous years.

For one thing, the declining birthrate we explained in the previous chapter means that there simply will be fewer adult children with whom an elderly parent can live. The parents of Boomers had an average of nearly four children; today's parents will have an average of fewer than two. Back at the turn of the century, about 65% of the unmarried elderly—with widowed women being the biggest single component—lived in the household of an adult child. Only about 10% lived alone. Today the numbers are reversed; about two-thirds of the unmarried elderly live alone. There is no indication that this trend will reverse itself in the next decade. In fact, with the growing financial independence among the elderly, the percentage of those living alone will continue to increase.

This seems to be borne out by the findings of a study conducted in 1988 by Transamerica Life Companies. Among middle-age persons (45 to 54 years old), 35% said that they plan to move to another home as soon as they retired. Among all middle-age and senior respondents, including those 65 and over, about half said they would like to live close to their children, but only 4% said they wanted to live *with* their children. Another interesting point brought out in the study was that among those 65 and older, 25% of them have adult children living in their homes, while only 18% are living in the homes of their adult children. The senior citizens also indicated that they felt financially secure. An astounding 91% said that they were completely or somewhat satisfied with their current standard of living.

Another factor discouraging seniors from moving in with their adult children is that the younger families have far more mobility. Many of them don't even live in the same states as their elderly parents, not to mention under the same roof. Seniors tend to root themselves and shy away from the nomadic lives of their career-seeking children.

This whole set of circumstances involving the elderly generates a multitude of opportunities for those who offer the right services. Foremost on the list of these services is health care. Health care is high on the list of services that are disproportionately consumed by those 65 and older. As a person gets older the need for health care and related services also tends to increase. A study by the Urban Institute has estimated that 18% of those over 65 need help in at least one basic daily activity, which includes dressing, eating, bathing, going to the bathroom, or getting in and out of bed or a chair. This indicates a tremendous need for providing personal services. Family members will provide them in some cases, but outside providers will be needed for most. We anticipate increased demand for various kinds of food services, laundry services, transportation and social activities. An ideal service of the 1990s and beyond would be one in which nutritionally proper meals would be delivered to homebound elderly persons. This might even be combined with simple laundry and house-cleaning services. There is a cost for these services, but it must be compared with the usually higher cost of having the elderly person move into a nursing home or other extended care facility.

Serving Healthy Seniors

One of the weaknesses that business has demonstrated over recent years is a misguided stereotyping of senior citizens. They do not make up one homogeneous group. There is a vast difference between a retired, affluent 65-year-old in good health and an 85-year-old living in an extended care facility. But advertising and marketing people often lump them into one tidy group. Author Ken Dychtwald devoted the bulk of his best-selling *Age Wave, The Challenges and Opportunities of an Aging America* to the proposition that American business has ignored senior citizens as a market, has insulted them with its advertising and has missed many opportunities to develop profitable products and services.

One category often overlooked is the "young senior" group, those 50 and over who are sometimes lumped into the same demographic senior citizen category. Perhaps one of the reasons for this is that the giant American Association of Retired Persons gleefully sends membership applications to people as soon as they reach their 50th birthday. That is offensive to many active 50-year-olds who don't consider themselves as falling into the "retired persons" market that the AARP serves. Although some working Americans may be shocked or chagrined at being invited to join the retirement association, the pitch apparently works. The AARP, with 30 million members, reputedly is second in size only to the Catholic church. Its magazine, *Modern Maturity,* has surpassed traditional magazines *TV Guide* and *Reader's Digest* to become the most widely distributed publication in the country, with a circulation at last count of 18 million.

To understand the over-50 market you must first appreciate its buying power. The group represents 49.5% of the nation's discretionary spending and an even bigger proportion of its wealth. Of course, this is not really the "retired" generation. Many of these people, in fact, are at the top of their trades or professions, and they are the most conspicuous consumers of a raft of luxury items ranging from expensive cars with cellular telephones to fancy health club memberships. But even if we looked at the over-65 market alone we would see a segment that accounts for 18% of the nation's discretionary spending. This is a market often ignored or misread by consumer products companies. While they don't spend as much per capita as the 50–64 age group, the over-65s are far different from the previous generation in this age group. For one thing, they generally are in better health and are more affluent than their predecessors. They eat out more often, attend more entertainment events and travel more. They even invest more and gamble more than the over-65 crowd did in the old days.

Marketers who are interested in the 50-and-over age group have many opportunities to capitalize on the growth in the market. One area is in clothing, which the fashion industry has aimed disproportionately at the youth market. Most mature American men can't cram their ample bodies into the typical Giorgio Armani suit. And most mature women prefer to pass on the thigh-high miniskirts that designers are always trying to push into common use. Opportunity is ripe for clothing stores to sell fashionable apparel to these young seniors. But the trend should start with Giorgio and his colleagues designing clothing lines specifically for young seniors.

More mature consumers also eat more conservatively than teenagers—fewer chili dogs and more tuna salad sandwiches. The oncoming expansion in the mature market should create opportunities for fast-food operations that are not geared toward the kiddie market. Most of the fast-food fare on the market today must be shunned by mature consumers trying to cut down on calories, cholesterol and other nutritional time bombs. Seniors also need different kinds of financial services than young people do, and the amount of their financial resources should attract banks and other institutions to develop new services for them. And travel is another area in which seniors can be better served. If we have Club Med for the young swingers, then there should be room for Club Medic for the older crowd. They want vacations that are a little quieter, engage in less strenuous activities, provide milder food and are close to a ready supply of Maalox.

The Rise in Age Power

As we progress down the road to 2000, the over-65s will grow slowly. But in the early years of the twenty-first century, when the Baby Boomers hit 65, this segment will explode into the biggest senior citizen market the country has ever seen. But this age group will wield more than monetary power; they also will have more political clout than any other senior group in history. Records consistently show that older citizens are far more likely to vote than younger citizens. For example, among retirees about 68% cast their votes in the 1984 presidential election, compared with 41% of those in the 18-to-24 age group. As our population ages, this factor will make it all the more difficult to enact any changes in Social Security. Congress will find it extremely difficult to make even the slightest alterations in the benefits provided by Social Security. This may develop into one of the major political problems of the coming decade. By the following decade, the Social Security problem may rank equally with the federal budget deficit.

There is widespread belief that older citizens tend to be more conservative and that the coming years will be marked by more conservative American politics. Not everyone agrees. A study conducted by Stephen Cutler, sociology professor of the University of Vermont, indicated that people do not become more conservative as they get older. Senior citizens change their attitudes and opinions just as readily as young people. The same study also maintained that seniors are not more set in their ways than the young. You cannot predict a person's sociopolitical outlook based on age, the report concluded. Educational attainment is a far better indicator.

As far as the so-called conservative bent of the country is concerned, we would agree that older people have not made the difference. The major change has been among younger people, all the way down to college students, more of whom have displayed more conservative political views in the past ten years. We also would suggest, although we know of no data to prove it, that people are more likely to change their political views in their 20s and 30s than they are in their 60s and 70s. As with many other generalities, we are not saying that people are more conservative but that more people are classified as conservative. There is a big difference. Similarly, when we say that people are growing older, we don't mean to say that our lifetimes will be pushed to more than 100 years. We are saying that more people will live to be senior citizens.

While a shift to an older population will bring many severe socioeconomic problems in the coming years, there also may be some hidden benefits. For one thing, the crime rate will probably decline. Of all persons arrested for serious crimes in the nation, nearly three-fourths are under the age of 25. Those 55 and over account for only about 3% of the arrests. The nation's highways also will be safer. Those over 55 account for about 25% of licensed drivers but make up only 15% of drivers involved in fatal accidents. They make up an even smaller proportion, 6%, of fatal accidents involving drunk drivers. One interesting footnote is that drivers under the age of 21, who cannot legally drink in the vast majority of states, account for nearly 25% of the fatal accidents involving drunk drivers.

The one remaining question is whether senior citizens, as they begin to dominate our population percentagewise, will do what the young did when they were in that position. As we recounted early in this chapter, the youth movement of the 1960s was marked with riots, protests and civil disturbances. Somehow we don't feel that the older folks will go to such lengths to have their voices heard. They won't have to. By 2000, those over the age of 48 will account for more than half of the registered voters in the country. All they will have to do is vote to make their wishes known.

FUTURE SCOPE

=== ADVISORY ===

Trends

- The median age of Americans is 33, the oldest ever recorded, and it will advance even more in the 1990s.

- The 65-and-over age cohort will explode in 2012 when Baby Boomers hit retirement age.

- Medical advances and improved fitness will allow more Americans to live longer lives.

- Despite greater longevity, Americans are retiring at a younger age.

- Retired Americans increasingly live alone rather than move in with their married children.

- The rapidly growing 35-and-over age group will dominate the ballot box in coming years. By 2000, half of all voters will be 48 and older.

Strategies

- Government will have to restructure Social Security to compensate for the growing imbalance between retired people and workers.

- Sales, profits and jobs in the health care industry will expand as the number of older people accelerates.

- The demand for retirement home and nursing home space will double in the next few years.

- Marketers should develop products, fashions and services that will appeal to an older, more affluent audience.

CHAPTER 4

The Land of Immigrants

There are more than 50 million Americans who are fully or partially of English descent, which is nearly as much as the population of the United Kingdom. There are more than 49 million Americans whose ancestors came to this country from Germany, which is more than half the combined population of West Germany and East Germany. There are about 40 million Americans who are of Irish ancestry, which is 12 times the population of the Republic of Ireland.

These figures demonstrate vividly that the United States is one huge nation of immigrants and their descendants. The force of immigration was evident during the early days of exploration and colonization of America. The Spanish, British and French all staked claims to parts of this continent.

But even then, immigration wasn't new to these shores. Reportedly, the Vikings landed here centuries before Christopher Columbus. Even earlier than that, the ancestors of American Indians are believed to have migrated here from Asia. Over the years our society was developed from this continuous supply of immigrants arriving here from different parts of the world. This flow of immigrants continues to this day, and indications are strong that it will increase throughout the coming decade. Indeed, immigration in the 1980s turned out to be at its highest level since the first decade of the twentieth century. Between 1901 and 1910, more immigrants came into the country than in any other period in U.S. history, averaging nearly 900,000 a year.

We started the century with a population of 76 million persons. During the first decade, 8.8 million immigrants were admitted to the country, representing more than 10% of our population at the time. Imagine what would happen to our country today if we admitted that same percentage of immigrants. It would represent 25 million newcomers. The following table shows immigration totals for the United States over the past century:

Decade	No. of Immigrants	Decade	No. of Immigrants
1871–1880	2,812,000	1931–1940	528,000
1881–1890	5,247,000	1941–1950	1,035,000
1891–1900	3,688,000	1951–1960	2,515,000
1901–1910	8,795,000	1961–1970	3,322,000
1911–1920	5,736,000	1971–1980	4,493,000
1921–1930	4,107,000	1981–1990	6,000,000 est.

One unusual aspect of the immigration is our collective attitude toward our countries of origin. Most of us—even though we were born here—still identify ourselves as being of immigrant stock. And it doesn't matter if our families have lived in the United States for generations. At least, that's what research shows. The number of German-Americans, Irish-Americans and English-Americans (We don't use that term very often, do we?) mentioned at the beginning of this chapter come from the 1980 "long form" census questionnaire. In analyzing the answers, the government's population counters found that only 6% of this country's residents identified their ancestry as "American." Isn't there something ironic about that? Here we are, approaching the 500th anniversary of the discovery of America, and the huge majority of American citizens still identify with their Old World roots. Some might see that as a weakness in our society. Others would say the diversity of backgrounds has made us stronger. If the latter is the case, then we are going to be even stronger in the future, because the immigration will continue and the mix of nationalities will expand. The primary difference, however, is that the new immigrants to this land are not coming from the same countries that provided our immigrants of 50, 100 and 200 years ago.

When you combine these new immigration patterns with the different birthrates of various ethnic groups, it becomes clear that the ethnic mix of our population is going to change. Not that there can be any rapid shift in only one decade. Our total population is so large it will take time to make profound changes in our ethnic mix. Nonetheless, the seeds of those changes are being planted right now and some of the results will inevitably come to fruition in the early years of the twenty-first century.

One thing is certain. In the next decade and, even more so, in the next century the average skin color of the American population—if it were possible to derive an average—will be a few shades darker than it is today.

The Browning of America

The single biggest source of immigrants to the United States in the past century has been Mexico, and the reason for this is fairly obvious. The United States is a wealthy country only a stone's throw across the Rio Grande from Mexico, which is mired in poverty. Many American employers—especially farm operators in the western states—need cheap labor, and Mexican immigrants can fulfill that need. Although this situation has existed for decades, the tempo of Mexican immigration has speeded up in recent years and probably will accelerate even more in the next decade. The prime cause for this is the Mexican economy, which can't create jobs fast enough to keep pace with its working-age residents.

Like the United States, Mexico had its own baby boom—fueled by a high fertility rate—in the 1950s, 1960s and 1970s. The country's population soared during those years, sometimes at a rate of more than 3% a year. Population grew from 53 million in 1970 to an estimated 89 million in 1990. Population growth has since slowed to a more modest 2.2% a year, but the total is still estimated to be more than 109 million as we enter the new century. Meanwhile, the number of Mexican Baby Boomers reaching working age is expanding at nearly twice the population growth rate.

As is the case in most developing countries, young people are leaving the rural areas to move to big cities. In this particular case, Mexico City is *the* big destination, as evidenced by its explosive growth. With more than 20 million residents, Mexico City today ranks as the largest urban center in the world. Back in 1960, it had a population of only 5.2 million and was the 13th largest metropolitan area in the world. Its population quadrupled in 30 years. Demographers estimate that over the next decade Mexico City's population will grow to nearly 26 million, which is almost as many residents as live today in California, our most populous state. By 2000 Mexico City's population will outrank Tokyo's by more than five million. Here is the record of Mexico City's march to the top:

City	1960	1970	1980	1990 (proj.)	2000 (proj.)
			(In millions)		
Mexico City	5.2	9.1	14.5	20.3	25.8
Tokyo	10.7	14.9	17.7	19.3	20.2
São Paulo	4.8	8.2	12.8	18.8	24.0
New York	14.2	16.3	15.6	15.7	15.8
Shanghai	10.7	11.4	11.8	12.4	14.3
Calcutta	5.6	7.1	9.5	12.5	16.5
Bombay	4.2	6.0	8.5	11.8	16.0
Buenos Aires	6.9	8.6	10.1	11.7	13.2
Seoul	2.4	5.4	8.5	11.7	13.8
Rio de Janeiro	5.1	7.2	9.2	11.4	13.3
Los Angeles	6.6	8.4	9.5	10.5	11.0
London	10.7	10.6	10.3	10.4	10.5

Analysts say the Mexican economy will have to create jobs at a rate of more than a million a year to provide employment for those coming of age. It is creating jobs at only about half that rate. Where are these jobless Mexicans going to find work? There is no question that they will flock here in even greater numbers than in the past.

But let's put that prediction into perspective. Between 1981 and 1985, more than 335,000 Mexicans entered the United States legally as permanent residents, which is the official definition of an

immigrant. This is 30,000 more than the number of immigrants arriving here from all European countries combined. This is a far cry
from the situation in the 1960s, when Europe was the source of more
than 1.2 million immigrants, while Mexico provided 443,000.

There is another element that adds to the significance of the growth
in Mexican immigration. We cannot ascertain how many Mexicans
are entering the country illegally or taking up permanent residence
after entering for what was to be a temporary period of time. Some
estimates suggest that this might add 25% or more to the legal immigration figures. One study by Census Bureau demographers estimated that 559,000 Mexicans entered the United States illegally
between 1975 and 1980 which, if accurate, would turn out to be nearly
twice the number who immigrated legally.

Mexico, though, isn't the only source of growing numbers of
Hispanic immigrants to the United States. An increasing number of
immigrants have been arriving here from South America and Central America, especially Colombia, Ecuador, Guyana, El Salvador
and Peru. Add to this the newcomers from the Caribbean region,
especially the Dominican Republic, and the total Hispanic immigration during the 1981–1985 period climbs to more than 800,000. (Not
included in any of these figures, of course, is the number of Puerto
Ricans who have moved to the mainland. They are not immigrants
because Puerto Rico is a commonwealth, and anyone born on the
island is automatically a citizen of the United States.)

Mexico also isn't the only Latin American country with a rapidly
growing population, as you can see from the preceding table. Back
in 1950, the total population of Mexico, Central America and South
America was 165 million, approximately the same as the combined
total for the United States and Canada. By 1985, however, the Latin
American population had soared to 405 million, while the United
States and Canada totaled only 264 million. Projections from the
United Nations indicate that by 2025, there will be twice as many
Latin Americans as Americans and Canadians.

Although there is a certain level of concern from some sources
about the Hispanic influx into the United States, this immigration
is serving the same purpose as did the huge European immigration
wave during the first decade of this century. The new immigrants
will join the pool of inexpensive labor that will fill the jobs being

created by American industry. They will be especially welcome to employers in the next decade because of the labor shortage caused by the dip in native-born Americans coming of working age. A study conducted for the National Bureau of Economic Research indicates that the influx of immigrants into a market usually has little impact on the income or employment of native-born Americans. Average salaries tend to slip a little in areas that are heavy in immigrants, but that is because immigrants generally are paid lower wages.

The Birthrate Factor

Immigration alone, however, will not be the only cause of growth in the Hispanic population. Most Hispanic ethnic groups have higher birthrates than the native American population. A U.S. Census Bureau report speculated that even if there were no Hispanic migration to the United States for the next 100 years, the Hispanic population would continue to grow at twice the national rate. Add the increased immigration to the higher birthrate and the result is a Hispanic population that is growing *three* times as fast as the non-Hispanic population. Conservative projections estimate that the nation's Hispanic population will double within 30 years. But the highest projections from the U.S. Census Bureau say that the Hispanic population could double within 12 years. In about 2020, the Hispanic share of the total U.S. population will surpass 14%, up from the current 8%. Somewhere between 2015 and 2020 the Hispanic population will surpass the black population for the first time in history.

Blacks, who make up about 12% of the total U.S. population, have a higher birthrate than the white population, but the black birthrate is declining along with the white. In coming years, whites will account for a smaller proportion of the total population and blacks will grow moderately, while the Hispanic share increases dramatically.

This Hispanic population boom may well have a profound impact on some major institutions in the next decade; one such institution is Congress. Because the Hispanic population is concentrated in only a few states, some observers say that Hispanics could capture as many as a dozen additional seats in the House of Representatives by 2000. This will help the ethnic group begin to make up for its underrepresentation in the political process. It can happen, though, only if Hispanics take a more active role in the voting process.

Another institution that will be affected by the trend is the Roman Catholic church. The great majority of Hispanics moving to the United States are Catholics. Projections indicate that Hispanics will make up about half of all Catholics in the United States by 2000. A decade after that, however, they will account for a solid majority of all Catholics in the country. This will create challenges and perhaps even problems for the church, which has been run by a largely European-American hierarchy throughout the history of the United States. At the same time, the expansion of the Hispanic population will give more political influence to the Catholic church in the twenty-first century.

The Asian Influx

If we looked at growth in percentage terms alone, we would see another minority group increasing even faster than blacks or Hispanics. The number of Asian-Americans in the United States grew by 142% in the 1970s and 58% in the 1980s. It is projected to grow by another 38% in the 1990s. We must remember, however, that Asians still make up less than 2% of the total U.S. population. But their total numbers will double in the next 20 years, and by the middle of the twenty-first century, Asian-Americans will have as large a share of our population as Hispanics have today. Because the Asian population in the United States is so small, the group is not tracked by census surveys as closely as blacks and Hispanics. The other problem is that the definition of *Asian* used by demographers is a catch-all category that includes everything from Turks to Pacific Islanders. Nonetheless, there is plenty of evidence to suggest that the Asian influence among the U.S. population will grow.

Most of the disproportionate growth in the Asian category has come about because of sharply higher immigration in the past couple of decades. Also adding to the influx of the past 20 years were more than 700,000 refugees from Southeast Asia. In 1960, for example, fewer than 100 immigrants came to the United States from Vietnam, Laos and Cambodia combined. In 1975, after the fall of Saigon, the country admitted more than 125,000 Vietnamese and Cambodians.

In terms of numbers, Asia now provides more immigrants to the United States than any other continent. In fact, in the 1980s immigration from Asia was more than four times as high as that from Europe. That is a reversal from the 1960s, when we were receiving three times as many immigrants from Europe as from Asia, largely due to government restrictions on the number of immigrants from Asia.

There is no one Asian country dominating the immigration rolls. The Philippines provide the highest number of immigrants. In fact, the Philippines are second only to Mexico as country of origin for immigrants. Substantial numbers also come from Korea, China (both Mainland and Taiwan), India, Laos and Iran.

For many years, Japanese-Americans were the largest Asian minority group in the United States, but they were overtaken by Chinese-Americans in 1980. Filipino-Americans, who increased their numbers by 62% in the 1980s, have since moved into the top position and, based on demographic projections, will probably stay on top.

With such small real numbers when compared with the white, black and Hispanic populations, one might think that Asian-Americans would have little impact on American life. That isn't the case. For one thing, Asians—just like Hispanics—have concentrated in only a few states. About 35% of all Asian-Americans live in California; and according to the intended place of residence listed by prospective immigrants, that state will maintain its high proportion. Another 40% of Asian-Americans live in only four states: Hawaii, New York, Illinois and Washington. Nowhere is the impact of immigration being felt more than in California. Over the next decade, two-thirds of the state's population increase will be Hispanic or Asian. In the late 1980s, Asians outnumbered blacks in California for the first time in history. Sometime during the first decade of the twenty-first century, we predict that non-Hispanic whites will turn into a minority in the state, a situation that already exists in Los Angeles County.

The influx of immigrants will create great demand for educational services, especially for English classes and job training courses. We expect that some companies will provide or underwrite such education as a means of attracting workers in a labor-shortage economy.

A Different Breed of Immigrant

Asian immigrants are remarkably different from the European immigrants that came here 75 years ago, and even from the Mexican immigrants that are flocking to the United States right now.

At the base of the Statue of Liberty is a well-known sonnet written by Emma Lazarus. In the sonnet, the statue — called the "Mother of Exiles" — beckons to immigrants with the famous words: "Give me your tired, your poor/your huddled masses yearning to breathe free. . . ." For more than a century that monument has welcomed immigrants to these shores, and those words aptly described the newcomers. They were fleeing their native countries because of war, poverty, oppression and hopelessness. They were on the bottom rung of their countries' social ladders and were coming to the new land because it offered them an opportunity they didn't have in their native countries.

Can you imagine how desperate they were to want to journey to the United States? There was no radio, television or movies when the bulk of Europeans migrated here after the turn of the century. Only through word of mouth did they have any notion of what the United States was all about. Most of them probably hadn't even seen a photograph of an American scene before they came here; nor could they read about this country because many were illiterate.

There also were no airplanes to transport them here in a few hours. They came in ships, tossed by the waves as they traveled for days. And most of them didn't luxuriate in first class, either. They came the cheapest possible way, these people. They were the new Americans, mostly poor and uneducated. And when they came here they went to work in the mills and mines, the fields and factories. Many of them never got an education, but the lucky ones saw their grandchildren go to college. They were the tired, the poor, the huddled masses. And that's why the new wave of immigrants, the Asian-Americans, are so different. While many of them came here in poverty, refugees from political strife in their own lands, many others were children of the wealthy. They attended college or graduate school in the United States and liked the country so much they decided to stay.

The basic difference with Asian-Americans is that they tend to be more highly educated than any other immigrant group. Nowhere is this more evident than among immigrants from India. Among U.S. residents 25 and over who were born in India, 66% have college degrees (among Taiwanese, 60%; among Filipinos, 42%; Koreans, 34%; Mainland Chinese, 30%). Compare these with European immigrants of the same age level living in the United States: Germans, 15%; Irish, 9%; Italians, 5%. Among the Mexican immigrants living here, only 3% have college degrees. It's obvious that these Asian immigrants aren't the huddled masses. They aren't on the bottom but the top rung, the best and brightest of their countries' populations. They are making their homes here not for survival, but for success.

In addition to outstripping other immigrant groups, Asian-American educational levels are also far higher than those reached by our total population, native born and foreign born. Among all U.S. residents 25 and over, only 20% have completed four years of college. Among blacks, 11% completed college, while among Hispanics—native born and immigrants—9% have four or more years of college. This doesn't speak well for the American educational system, but more than that it doesn't speak well for the value that native-born Americans place on a college education. And the problem isn't an economic one; the majority of Americans can afford some kind of higher education, if not at a major university then at a junior or community college. Virtually anyone can work his or her way through college if he or she has the desire to move ahead. Educational trends do not bode well for blacks or Hispanics, the two largest minority groups, both of which are severely underrepresented in college enrollment. The share of students from those ethnic groups is not only below average but has declined significantly in the past decade, even though the percentage of white students going on to college has increased.

This is an important indicator for the future. The fewer minority members attending college today, the fewer minority professionals there will be in the next decade.

Blacks Falling Behind

The situation among blacks is particularly distressing to educators. A study by the Center for Demography and Ecology at the University of Wisconsin reports that the proportion of black high school graduates going on to college declined from 48% in 1977 to

38% in 1983. The percentage started to inch upward in the past couple of years, but the gain came only among upper-income blacks. Among poorer blacks – those most in need of more education – the percentage apparently continues to decline. The primary reason put forth for the decline in black college enrollment were the cutbacks in financial aid aimed at minorities. That may be a factor, but it is simplistic to place all the blame on government agencies. There is no question that going to college is not even considered by a significant percentage of blacks. Of all college-bound high school students taking the Scholastic Aptitude Test (SAT) and the American College Testing (ACT) program, fewer than 8% are black.

This is more a matter of cultural deprivation than lack of money. Many black youngsters are brought up in homes where there is no tradition of higher education and often no family encouragement to go on to college. Without the desire and determination, it will be extremely difficult for any black youngster to attain a higher socioeconomic level. Poverty adds to the difficulty. So does the reality that at many inner-city high schools, as many as half of the students drop out before receiving their diplomas. Even those black students who graduate from high school often receive inferior educations in big-city school systems. They have little chance of competing against white students coming out of suburban, private and parochial school systems. This whole situation is a problem that the federal government has ignored in the past decade. And no other institution, public or private, seems capable of solving it.

Asian-Americans obviously value education more highly than the rest of our population. If that disparity in values continues, then the next decade should show Asian-Americans moving to the top in business, the professions and the arts. That trend has already started to show itself. Asian-Americans earn a disproportionately high percentage of the doctorate degrees awarded by American universities. In engineering, for example, Asian-Americans account for about 15% of all doctorates awarded to American citizens. This does not include foreign students from Asia studying in this country under temporary visas. Of some concern to educators is the fact that the percentage of doctorates going to U.S. citizens is declining. Americans account for only about 72% of doctorate degrees from U.S. universities, down from 86% in 1962.

Asian-Americans, meanwhile, have displayed a high level of virtuosity in such areas as classical music. Their representation among the nation's best symphony orchestras is bound to increase greatly in the next ten years. Filipino-Americans have a disproportionately high level of participation in the medical field. At the same time, large shares of Chinese, Korean and other Asians have moved into entrepreneurial areas of all sorts. Many of these enterprises are little more than mom-and-pop operations such as the manicure salons that have sprouted up recently in New York City. That business is rapidly being taken over by Korean-Americans, who operate about 450 salons in New York. They often finance these ventures by pooling their resources. Then they work industriously, live as inexpensively as possible and use the profits to start up other small businesses.

The Asian education and work ethic has already had positive results for many Asian ethnic groups. Except for the Vietnamese and Laotians — most of whom came here as refugees — every other Asian immigrant group has a higher proportion working in professional occupations than do native-born Americans.

These ethnic groups also have higher median household incomes than do native-born Americans or any other immigrant cohort. As with their leadership in education, Indian-Americans also have the highest median household income, more than 20% higher than native-born Americans.

Although a professional education is a key explanation for higher incomes among Asian-Americans, researchers have also found that these ethnic groups tend to have more members of their families at work, which adds to their income totals.

The Future of Discrimination

We can't talk about minorities in this country without discussing the prospects of discrimination and segregation. There has always been a tendency on the part of most immigrant groups to congregate in ghettos when they move into a new area. That was how ethnic neighborhoods formed in American cities in the nineteenth and twentieth centuries. Blacks moving from the rural South to the industrialized North were virtually the same as immigrants, and they, too, moved into ghettos. Hispanics and various Asian groups also are moving into newer ghettos in the big cities, although some of them may not be as blighted as the older black ghettos.

Several studies have indicated that Asians will be able to move more rapidly into mainstream America than blacks and Hispanics. There has been little resistance against Asians, especially professionals, moving into suburban areas and upscale city neighborhoods. This is largely the result of their high socioeconomic position. In the decade to come the more affluent and more highly educated Asians should have little trouble assimilating into basically white mainstream America.

The challenge will be greater for Hispanics, although once again, socioeconomics will have a lot to do with acceptance. Hispanics who can afford to move out of their ghettos into predominantly white areas generally will not face much resistance (although there are always pockets of bigots who will resist any newcomers). Publications in California, which has the largest concentration of Hispanic immigrants, have already begun writing about the "brown elite," Hispanics who have moved into upper-income levels and have started to make their influence felt. The important lesson that non-Hispanics in various cities will have to learn is that Hispanics come from many different cultures and backgrounds, even though they speak a common language. They are not a single ethnic group that acts, thinks and votes the same way.

The greatest problem in terms of discrimination and segregation will continue to be faced by black Americans. In fact, native-born American blacks might even face more discrimination than blacks from Africa or the West Indies. Unlike bias leveled at Asians and Hispanics, discrimination against blacks appears to be based on more than a difference in socioeconomics. Even though the movement promoting desegregation and equality of opportunity for blacks has been pushing ahead for decades, their progress will continue to come more slowly than for other minorities.

Just as with other ethnic groups, blacks are not a monolithic social unit but a series of subgroups. One of these is a small emerging upper class of blacks—second- and third-generation professionals—who circulate in upper-class white circles. There also is a growing black middle class with more limited interaction with the white middle class. These groups, a minority within their own minority, are pulling away from the great mass of blacks who are trapped in the poverty-welfare cycle. This will create deeper divisions in the coming years between the haves and have-nots in the black community.

The decline in the number of blue-collar jobs generated by our economy in the next decade will make it more difficult for poorly educated blacks to find a path out of the ghetto. It was the good-paying factory jobs that allowed many black families to send their children to college, giving them an opportunity that their parents didn't have. Without the ready supply of blue-collar jobs, and without the traditional family value placed on education, many blacks are going to remain mired in a lower class that isn't participating in the American dream.

Overall, however, blacks have better opportunities today than they did at the end of World War II. Most institutionalized segregation has been eliminated, at least technically. Ritual discrimination against blacks is not as prevalent as it was 40 years ago, except among lower-class whites who are threatened by anyone who might bypass them on the social ladder.

We see no end to the radical rhetoric of fringe groups such as the Skinheads, Ku Klux Klan and other neo-Nazi organizations. The fact that they are even making their shrill noises is evidence that blacks are making social and economic progress in our society.

When we reach 2000, however, we probably will find that Asians and Hispanics — despite language difficulties and despite being relative newcomers to our society — will have made more progress than most blacks in achieving some measure of equality in the American society.

In the 1990s, the United States will continue to be the melting pot that it was throughout the twentieth century. But we detect some changes in Americans who have been here for two or more generations. When the descendants of immigrants start moving out of their ghettos, their aim is usually to assimilate into the American culture. They try to look, act and talk like the rest of American society. Many will attempt to suppress the culture of the country from which their immigrant parents came. But a generation or two down the road, their children who have become "real" Americans often try to reconnect with their national heritage. They search out their family roots, study the language of their grandparents, visit the "old country" and try to recapture a bit of the culture. They aren't regressing. Like generations before them they want to be part of American society. But they find that the more they become like everyone else, the more they try to find those features that will distinguish them from the rest.

ADVISORY

Trends

- Immigration is approaching record levels of the early 1900s.

- The fastest-growing minority in total numbers are Hispanics. With high birthrate, Hispanic population will double in 30 years and surpass the black population.

- Asian immigrants are growing at the fastest percentage increase. Their population will double in 20 years.

- Most Asian ethnic groups have higher educational levels than native-born Americans.

- The percentage of blacks and Hispanics going to college is declining. They will struggle to fill more demanding jobs of the 1990s.

- The gap is widening between middle-class and disadvantaged blacks.

Strategies

- Demand will grow for English classes and job training for immigrants.

- Congress and the states will have to respond to the influx of Hispanics, who are underrepresented at all government levels.

- Public education systems will have to be radically upgraded to help inner-city Americans break out of the ghettos.

- Marketers should cater to the growing influence of Hispanic and Asian food, fashions and customs.

CHAPTER 5

The New American Family

Ever so often, a social philosopher — whether of the professional or the cracker-barrel variety — will decry the deterioration of the American family. In no particular order, the blame for this predicament is placed on the federal government, communism, the media, a decline in religious practice or rock and roll music. Looking at this with a healthy dose of skeptical objectivity, one should recognize that families are made up of human beings. And human beings are no better or worse today than they were 50 years ago. We can only assume that the same observation holds for families.

One thing that is definite about both families and individuals is that they are vastly different today from what they were 50 years ago, or even ten years ago. Like everything else, they are in a constant state of flux, responding to the changes in the world around them, and forcing other institutions to adapt to them. Because of this we know one other definite fact as we tiptoe into the 1990s: Families will function differently ten years from now as they cross over into the twenty-first century. Our challenge is to anticipate how families and home life will be different and to determine how to respond to that difference.

The reasons for all of this constant change are complex. As a social unit, the family traditionally was counted on to perpetuate the human race. That duty apparently was more important in an earlier day than it is in American society today. We no longer have to sire children in order to make our tribe more powerful (although some social critics believe that the leveling off of our population will make us a less influential nation).

In the past, the family served as a protective device for each of its members, but especially for the women and children. The bigger the family, the better it could protect its own. In some cultures, raising a large brood of children was considered a form of social security. The more children you had, the more there would be to take care of you in your old age. In today's society, vestiges of these family-building motivations may still echo, but not very loudly. The role of the family has undergone some dramatic changes. Most Americans no longer feel pressured to have large families for protection or financial security. More than that, the ready availability of birth control methods has given American parents positive control over their own parenthood. They can determine how many children they will have and when they will have them. Married couples today can plan for a child in the same way they might plan a European vacation. They build up their financial resources in advance and even time the event so that it doesn't interfere with the career paths of mother or father.

As a result of all of these changes, the reasons Americans have children have also shifted. To be sure, there are still some for whom raising a family is a religious or social obligation. They might shun birth control measures, leaving the matter of parenthood to nature and chance. And they might believe that the more children they have, the more blessed they will be. This outlook toward family is certainly more traditional and may even be considered Old World — inspired by some social progressives. We aren't here to judge the merits of various family practices, but we do want to trace the trends having an impact on families. Although statistics are not available, we must assume by the declining birthrate that the numbers of Americans who follow the traditional ways are shrinking.

One thing that has not declined in recent years is the number of children born to unmarried women. The number in fact has soared, quadrupling from about 225,000 in 1960 to nearly one million in the late 1980s. Having a child out of wedlock has become commonplace among black Americans. More than 60% of black babies are born to unmarried mothers, up from less than 38% in 1970. The percentage among whites born out of wedlock is lower, about 15% currently, but is rising at a faster rate. Back in 1970, only 5.7% were born out of wedlock, and in 1960 only 2.3%. What consternates social workers is that the increase in illegitimate births corresponds with an increase in sex education, the availability of birth control measures and the legalization of abortion.

If a book like this had been written in 1960, it probably would have projected a sharp decline in illegitimate births by now. All of the factors and trends were pointing in that direction. Based on what has actually occurred, the projection would have been dead wrong. That should demonstrate how difficult it is to predict the future, even with so-called hard data in hand. But it also shows that internal motivations of human beings are more important than outside influences.

Experts in the field point out that the teen pregnancy rate in the United States is the highest among industrialized countries. This is not because American teenagers are more sexually active than teenagers in other countries. They aren't. But teenagers, especially those who are poor and uneducated, may have more difficulty getting contraceptive counseling here than their counterparts do in other countries. This should prompt those in power to reconsider the measures they have taken to reduce illegitimate births, especially to teenage mothers. The measures obviously have not worked.

The majority of unmarried men and women (and boys and girls) who are having babies today know what causes them and know how to prevent them. Since they aren't doing the latter, we can also assume that many of them want to have children; and there is a goodly amount of anecdotal evidence to back up that contention. Some teenage girls feel that having a baby is a sign of maturity, a rite of passage for them. Others look at motherhood as a way to escape school. In some areas, young girls believe it is an honor to have a baby sired by a particularly powerful gang member or other local hero, a view more prevalent among teenagers from disadvantaged backgrounds. Teenagers with low educational aspirations and weak career potential are also more likely to become sexually active earlier in life. The more advantaged, motivated kids take their time.

There is no question that drugs and alcohol, a lack of positive family influence and, in some cases, invincible ignorance have all contributed to the increase in illegitimate births among teenage girls. But we can't blithely wave off illegitimacy as just another juvenile problem. Illegitimacy is not limited to the young. It is important to recognize that illegitimate births among older women are increasing at a far faster rate than they are among teenagers. In fact, the share of illegitimate births by girls under 15 has declined to about 1%, down from 2.4% in 1970. The actual number of births to girls under 15 is close to 10,000 a year, which is about where it was in 1970.

Girls 15 to 19 account for about 32% of all illegitimate births, down from nearly 48% in 1970. The biggest increases are in women 20 years old and above. (Before you walk away believing that the problem of teenage pregnancy is being solved, remember that the primary reason for the slippage in percentage is that there were fewer teenagers in our population in the 1980s than there were in the 1970s.)

Adult women (20 and over) now account for more than 65% of births to unmarried mothers, compared with less than 50% in 1970. This increase fits in logically with other figures we have seen. Men and women are getting married later in life, which means that they stay single longer. This also means there is more opportunity to have a baby before marriage.

A Change in Values

The increase in births to unmarried adult women is also a result of shifts in values that started in the 1960s. One of these is the now well-developed trend of unmarried couples living together. Before the 1960s, most of American society frowned on unmarried couples of the opposite sex living together. Couples who lived together long enough were considered to be in a common-law marriage, a relationship associated largely with those in the lower socioeconomic strata.

By the 1960s, couples from more affluent families with higher educational levels and from more traditional backgrounds also started entering into live-in relationships. At the time, though, this was viewed by traditionalists as an act of antiestablishmentarianism; it was a sign of the rebellious times.

Over the past 25 years, living together has definitely moved into the mainstream among young adults. The number of unmarried-couple households increased by 117% in the 1970s, and another 63% between 1980 and 1988, when the total reached 2.6 million households. Among today's newlyweds, it has been estimated that 60% live together before tying the knot. Although the participants remain unmarried, many of these relationships last longer than some marriages. Indeed, the participants often think of themselves as essentially being married and many have children, contributing to the increased number of technically illegitimate children. Census Bureau figures indicate that 31% of unmarried-couple households have one or more children under age 15, and the percentage has edged upward through the past two decades. This doesn't mean that 31% of the unmarried couples have had their own children. In many cases, the children are the product of a previous marriage or live-in relationship with a different mate.

The other shift in values deals with the growing tolerance for out-of-wedlock births. Most segments of society still consider illegitimacy to be a breach of morals rather than a mere indiscretion. But fewer Americans look upon it as an ignominious stigma upon mother and child. This has added to the increased acceptance of out-of-wedlock births as "just one of those things."

There also are unmarried women—perhaps some who feel they will be among the growing numbers who will never marry—who want to have a child but not necessarily a husband. They don't account for a huge number of births, but they do contribute to the long-term attitude of acceptance toward illegitimacy.

Unless there is some kind of renewed moral backlash against illegitimacy in the 1990s—which is unlikely—it will continue to remain at historically high levels. There will be shifts in the age groups of unmarried women having babies simply because the numbers of women in these groups are shifting. As a result, we can expect to see teenage pregnancies pop up in the mid-1990s as the children of the Baby Boomers hit their early childbearing years. The percentage of births to unmarried women in their 20s will decline, a result of this decade's lower teenage population level.

One outside factor that might have an impact on these numbers by 2000 will come from leaders in the black community who are turning up the volume in their preaching against illegitimacy. Influences of this kind, however, seldom produce dramatic results. It usually takes decades to develop a significant response, if indeed there ever is one.

The Shrinking American Family

The most consistent trend that has been noted over the past 30 years is the declining size of the American family. Because this is a figure that includes most of our population, it can move only slowly; but the movement has been unrelenting. In 1960, the average American family had 3.67 members. This declined to 3.58 in 1970, 3.29 in 1980, and 3.17 in 1988. This is the smallest average family size ever recorded in the United States.

These are families, not households, and the distinction is important. The technical difference is that a family is two or more persons living in the same household who are related by birth, marriage or adoption. Households include all families as well as persons living alone and unrelated persons living together.

Because of the rapid growth of single-person households, average household size has diminished even faster than average family size. In 1960, the average American household had 3.33 members, which was nearly as large as the average family at that time. But this dropped to 3.14 in 1970, 2.76 in 1980, and 2.64 in 1988, also the smallest household size in history.

By now readers should realize that the declining birthrate is one of the reasons for the decline in family size. But it isn't the only reason. Another major factor is the increase in the number of single-parent households. By the late 1980s, more than 26% of all families with children under 18 were headed by single parents. This was up considerably from 19.1% in 1980 and 12.3% in 1970. In actual numbers, this represents about 15 million American kids who live with only one parent. Nearly 90% of these single-parent households are headed by women, and—despite all of the talk about equal rights and shared custody—there has been very little shift in that share over the past 20 years. Also adding to the decline in family size is the tendency of grandparents to set up their own households and not move in with their married children after retirement or widowhood.

This is the point at which people usually ask: "Whatever happened to the traditional American family? You know the one I mean—with

Mom, Dad and Junior." The answer is that the typical American family has become atypical. Here is how the numbers break down:

- There are close to 91.5 million households in the United States. Of these, about 26 million are nonfamily households, and about 85% of the nonfamily households are persons living alone.
- Of the remaining 65.5 million family households, 33.5 million have no children under 18. This means that a majority of the families in the country have no children at home, the first time that has ever occurred. These are mostly younger couples with no children or older couples—empty nesters—whose children have left home.
- Of the remaining 32 million families with children, nearly ten million are headed by single parents. That leaves about 22 million "typical" American families, representing only 24% of the households in the country.

One change we might have to make is our definition of *young married couples*. Because of later marriages, the number of married couples under the age of 25 declined by 38% between 1980 and 1988. When we examine all of these trends, one interesting fact pops up: Families in the next decade will experience a wider age gap between parents and children. We don't know if it is important, but it will exist.

A Different Kind of Family

A great deal of discussion and controversy concerns the diminishing importance of family life and a deterioration in family values. While some families and cultures have steadfastly maintained these values through the changes of the past few decades, there is no question that others have shunned them. Because we are dealing with human values and not with Census Bureau statistics, projecting the future course of these attitudes is an inexact science, to say the least. Some say that the decline in family values since World War II was caused in part by our rapid population growth, plus the increased concentration on acquiring wealth and possessions. Others, such as futurist Edward Cornish, see the beginning of a "singles society" since the proportion of single adults has climbed to an all-time high. The market for singles activities has already created many new business opportunities, from singles bars to dating services. But the real impact may come in the lessening of family influence on our society. Single people, for example, may not be as eager to support education as families are.

Despite that theory, we may be headed for a return to some of the traditional family values by the twenty-first century. The first point is that our population growth has slowed to a crawl. In addition, our largest age group—the ubiquitous Baby Boomers—is in its peak family-forming years. The sheer numbers of Boomer families might be enough to tilt the average family structure back to the way it was 30 years ago.

Another point that may affect the future of the family is the nation's growing conservatism, which is explored in another chapter. This does not mean, however, that we are going to return to the naive "Leave It to Beaver" days. There are some overriding trends that show no signs of letting up, such as the increase in working mothers and two-income households. Mom isn't going to spend the day at home making meat loaf. She will spend less time at the supermarket. Competent child care will be a primary concern of the 1990s. Families will be concerned over how to pay for the care of their elderly parents, but they will be less likely to welcome them into their homes than they did in previous generations.

By 2000 our society probably will start developing again what has become known as the "typical American family." But that ideal matrix will be far different from the typical family we remember from our youth.

The Home as Workplace

One of the trends that social scientists have been writing about in recent years is the home-based work movement. Because so many mothers are moving into the work force, it seems logical that many of them prefer to work at home, if possible, so they can also take care of their children. Working at home saves the family the cost of child care, plus it eliminates the time and cost of going back and forth to the job. If the work space in the home were handled properly, it also could be used as an income tax deduction by the homeworker.

A person who could work at home, therefore, would generally accept lower wages than one who must travel daily to an appointed workplace. This bit of reasoning corresponds with the needs of many employers who are looking for low-cost workers. In this age of a globalized economy, American employers must compete with Third World companies that have a ready supply of cheap labor.

Because providing work space for an employee costs money, home-based workers are more economical to have on the payroll. The practice would cut down on absenteeism, allow for employment of the handicapped, provide part-time jobs for senior citizens and even cut down on traffic congestion. Furthermore, these homeworkers don't even have to be employees. They can just as easily be outside contractors operating their own cottage industries. That would alleviate the need for health insurance, pension funds and other employee benefits.

Plenty of reasons make home-based work a commonsense work alternative for the 1990s. And the means to accomplish it are available in the implementation of technology that is already developed. The networking of personal computers through telephone lines would allow such labor-intensive functions as data entry to be performed off-premises. But the list of jobs that could be performed in the home run the gamut of activities from sewing to product assembly to computer programming.

Such renowned social philosophers as Alvin Toffler have predicted that homeworking would explode in the 1980s and 1990s. Dozens of books and hundreds of magazine articles have been written about it. Some have referred to the "electronic cottage" as the nation's homes that would be connected electronically to work centers. There has been only one flaw in this trend: It hasn't been as dramatic as the experts have predicted. There may be a few more people working in their homes, but the great movement toward corporate employees working at home and being linked by computer and telephone to their offices has not taken place in the 1980s, and there is little indication that it will explode in the 1990s.

What has increased is the number of home-based businesses, entrepreneurial operations that full-time workers or full-time household managers operate to augment their incomes. Among them are free-lance workers, such as artists and writers, and the expanding field of consultants. Estimates of the American home-based work force numbering 25 million is a bit misleading because they include these entrepreneurs as well as office-based employees who bring work home.

One reason the work-at-home movement has not exploded might be the controversy that has started to swirl around it. Critics maintain that the practice would create an invisible work force that could easily be exploited by business. There also have been questions raised about the potential violation of local zoning ordinances. But more than all of these, it appears that women—considered the most likely candidates for at-home work—don't want to be prisoners in their own homes. Physically going to work gives them a sense of mobility and freedom they wouldn't have at home. If they have to work to provide the family's second income, then they want to be able to have someone else care for their children. They also want the social contact that going to the workplace provides, which, for some workers, is as important as the income earned from the job. Social scientists will continue to talk about home-based work in the years ahead, but it might well be a concept whose time will never come.

Grazing Through the 1990s

One of the more definite trends in traditional American home life is the evolution of our dining patterns. In 1978 researchers Leo J. Shapiro and Dwight Bohmbach wrote an article in *Advertising Age* in which they identified the developing "grazing society" in America. There are heavy grazers and light grazers, but most of us are grazing more than ever before. The concept applies to the increase in eating meals outside the home. But the term *grazing* takes on its full significance when you consider the lifestyle of some heavy grazers. Take an unmarried young executive, who downs only a cup of coffee before leaving for work on a Monday morning. On the way to the job, he stops at the local McDonald's for an Egg McMuffin. Later on he takes a client out for a pricey expense-account lunch. After work he and a couple of colleagues go to the local sports bar for a beer and some snacks. He meets a young woman colleague in the bar and asks her to join him for dinner at a new Thai restaurant. We won't go into any further detail on that evening's activities.

On Tuesday, however, he has lunch in-flight while heading off on a business trip. He will spend the next three days at a convention, returning on Friday. He has a sandwich at his desk in order to catch up with the paperwork. Later that evening, he will stop at the sports bar again and order some barbecued ribs with a side of coleslaw to carry out.

On Saturday he runs out for a light breakfast at Dunkin' Donuts. He is going to the baseball game that day, where he will have two hot dogs, a bag of peanuts and an ice-cream bar, not to mention a couple of beers. On Sunday morning his mother will call and say that she hasn't seen him in a month and doesn't he want to come for dinner that day. He accepts.

This is a person who is grazing through life, the way a cow grazes through a grassy field. All of us know someone like this, the person whose refrigerator contains a six-pack of beer, an almost-empty jar of mustard, a jar of kosher dill pickles, a loaf of very old bread, a can of tuna, the remains of Friday's ribs and coleslaw, and the remnants of a long-forgotten meal that has long since turned green.

Our friend may be on the cutting edge of the grazing movement, but many of us can identify with some aspects of his food-on-the-run existence. And the statistics demonstrate conclusively that we are eating more meals away from the home. On any given day, about half of the American population eats at a restaurant or buys carryout food. The restaurant business, fueled largely by the growth in the fast-food sector, has soared in sales in the past 20 years. Restaurant sales jumped from about $22 billion in 1970 to $72 billion in 1980 to an estimated $150 billion in 1990.

These figures are for freestanding restaurants only and do not include hotel restaurants and institutional food service. In away-from-home dining, we must also include meals eaten at work and school, in hospitals, on airplanes, in clubs, at sporting events, at banquets and luncheons, at picnics and in prisons. We also must include in this category food prepared at another location but eaten in the home. This is an important part of the trend because it is the fastest-growing subcategory. Some estimates say that home delivery of prepared foods was growing at the rate of 30% a year in the late 1980s. There also were significant increases in carryout sales. Not included in this total, but certainly part of the trend, are microwavable meals sold at supermarkets and food stores. When you consider all meals eaten away from home or prepared outside the home, they account for more than 43% of the nation's food expenditures. In 1970, they accounted for only 29% of our food budget.

Just as important as the numbers are the attitudes of Americans toward their meals. Researchers point out that going out to a restaurant or buying carryout food was once considered an optional treat. With two-income households, however, coming home with a carryout meal is part of the lifestyle package—one of the elements that allows both partners to work.

As the grazing trend accelerates there also seems to be a blurring of the line between meals and snacks. People are less likely to sit down for a full formal meal; the one-and-only course might be pizza. A cocktail party with heavy hors d'oeuvres might make a sit-down dinner unnecessary. Restaurants have responded to this trend recently by serving smaller portions (although not necessarily at lower prices). One growing segment of the business is comprised of restaurants that serve only appetizer-size dishes.

What also is being blurred is the distinction between eating out and eating at home. As more dinners are being carried in, family members may sit down at a meal where everyone has his or her own requested dish for that evening. If Mom is stopping at the gourmet deli on the way home from work, she might as well buy what each family member wants. None of this bodes well for the future of items like family-size roasts, big hams, turkeys or legs of lamb. Once the staple of the American table, they will become items served only on rare occasions. Mom will no longer have the time to prepare such meals during the workweek.

In the next decade there will be a growing demand for dinner food that requires little or no preparation. Restaurants will battle supermarkets to become the main source of carryout food, and both will reap the benefits of the trend. There also will be an increase in the number and selection of food places that sell *only* carryout food. By 2000, the most important appliances in putting dinner on the table will not be the kitchen range or the food processor but the telephone and the car.

Aside from carryout, the restaurant business will continue to see modest to strong growth through the 1990s. This is not because everybody wants to or can afford to eat out more often but because the segment of our population that eats out most often are those in the 45–54 age group; and this will be the fastest-growing age segment over the next decade.

Born to Shop

Over the past 20 years, shopping has developed into an art form in the United States. It used to be a form of entertainment for many men and women, but that has changed as the demands on time have increased. As far as food shopping is concerned, we are making more trips to the supermarket, but shorter ones. The average supermarket visit takes about 20 minutes, ten minutes less than it did in the mid-1970s. This is going to create an unusual anomaly in the next decade.

The trend in supermarket size is definitely toward larger parcels of real estate. Twenty years ago, supermarkets ran in the range of 20,000 to 30,000 square feet. Those gradually grew into superstores that run from 40,000 to 60,000 square feet; but even they are dwarfed by the next generation of retail stores.

The next new entry will be the hypermarkets, a combination full-service supermarket and general discount store under a roof that can cover four football fields (a football field is 48,000 square feet). The concept originated in France many years ago but only recently came to the United States. If you want to compare the size of a hypermarket to your local supermarket, just consider that a Hypermart USA store in Dallas has 2,000 shopping carts and 52 checkout counters.

Even though supermarkets of the future are destined to be larger, American shoppers, especially those who work full-time outside of the home, are looking for speed and convenience. Hypermarkets can't provide these features for the time-driven shopper. They would appeal more to the retired customer or the full-time homemaker.

The larger food stores become, the more demand there will be for easy-in, easy-out convenience stores such as the 7-Eleven Food Store chain. This is particularly true for the person who doesn't want to shop at all but needs a specific item for a meal or for the home.

In the next decade, look for supermarket operators to try various techniques to attract customers looking for only a few items. One of these might be a drive-up window where you can get a gallon of milk or a loaf of bread, or pick up a telephoned-in order without leaving your car.

While demanding more speed, shoppers increasingly are telling researchers that they want to do all of their food buying in one location. They are less willing to scoot from one store to another to take advantage of a low-price special. As a result of this attitude, store loyalty is on the upswing. Half of the consumers questioned in a recent survey said that they did all of their shopping at one favorite store.

Supermarket operators would be well advised to establish a stronger relationship between store and customer, perhaps offering new services that might make shopping more convenient for customers. What is ironic is that most supermarkets—except for measuring the kinds of merchandise that people buy—don't have the slightest idea of what their customers want. They don't even have anything as fundamental as a list of names and addresses of their best customers. If they had that, they might be able to ask their customers how they could serve them better. There will be plenty of room in the 1990s for services that can make supermarkets better suppliers and more adroit marketers.

This is already happening as supermarkets are edging out of the conventional grocery trade into areas that offer a touch of convenience for their shoppers. A supermarket today might offer video rental, photo finishing, a florist shop and a Federal Express drop-off box. The most common extension has been into salad and soup bars, pizza, barbecued ribs and chicken and other items that fall into the carryout category. Supermarkets also are offering modest in-store dining for those who have to shop during their lunch hour.

As two-income families abound, the roles of husband and wife are shifting steadily, if not dramatically. As far as shopping habits are concerned, men and women are becoming more alike. Husbands are more likely to shop regularly for food and other household items, something previously considered a woman's chore. Working women who shop are also acquiring some of the characteristics associated with male shoppers. They are making more impulsive purchases; they are less likely to prepare a shopping list; they spend less time in the store; they are less likely to redeem coupons; they are less likely to read the store's ads; and they are less likely to read the newspaper that carries the ads.

This shifting of habits has been identified by consumer products companies as well as food retailers. The manufacturers say that at least two-thirds of the buying decisions on particular products are made at the point of sale. There has already been an escalation in the amount of in-store promotion, but we can expect it to grow even more in the next decade. The most evident vehicle — literally — will be the shopping cart. Several companies are selling advertising space on carts to food companies. There also will be greater use of advertising tied in with aisle-end displays.

Video monitors were installed at thousands of checkout counters a few years back to play commercials that consumers could watch while they waited in line. This idea bombed out, not only because consumers develop negative vibes when they have to wait in line, but also because it is useless to advertise to someone waiting to get out of the store. In the next ten years, retailers will develop the video monitor into a new profit center by using it more effectively.

Shoppers also will see electronic message boards attracting their attention to specific items on sale, as well as audio announcements on closed-circuit in-store broadcasts. The supermarket will appeal increasingly to people who don't watch television and don't read newspapers.

The Peaking of the Pleasure Dome

Having said all of this about the consumer's need for speedy shopping, we must add a few words about that twentieth-century mecca of merchandise, the shopping mall. We are projecting various trends and demands based on the fact that the number of working women and mothers is increasing. That is fact, and we can assume that someone will be meeting their needs. But there also are millions of Americans who are not working mothers, who are not married, who have no children and so forth. For many such persons, the shopping mall has become, as one business journal called it, the "pleasure dome" of suburban America. In some newer suburbs the local shopping mall is essentially the downtown area, the center of town. It is not only where the better stores are, but it also is where the teenagers hang out, especially at the fast-food eateries in the malls. Malls also provide a place where senior citizens can come in from the elements and browse in comfort. Attesting to their new roles as town centers some of the large, sprawling malls open their doors early in the morning for local folks to come in to do their fitness walking. Malls also present art shows, military displays, concerts, carnivals, Christmas caroling and many other kinds of community promotions.

Over the next decade, however, the growth in mall shopping will level off and may even decline. The lower number of teenagers today will translate into fewer young adults in the next decade.

Customers are increasingly shopping closer to where they work or where they live. As more potential shoppers take on full-time work, shopping malls will be more crowded in the evenings and on weekends, but far more quiet during the daytime. Customers working full-time are less likely to drive long distances unless they are on daylong shopping excursions. As with supermarkets, customers often have to make a quick trip for a specific item. They don't want to spend half of Saturday looking for a spot in the parking lot.

The 1990s customer also will be more likely to buy merchandise by mail order, telephone, direct response, catalog or computer. We say this realizing that some home-shopping efforts have been monumental failures. One of these was Telaction, an interactive shopping system that J. C. Penney Co. tested for a year through several Midwest cable television systems. Viewers were able to buy any of the clothing, housewares and groceries by punching codes into their pushbutton telephones. It will take more time before Americans are ready to buy a wide variety of merchandise from home. We can't imagine even the busiest woman, for example, buying a dress from a television screen without trying it on or touching the fabric. The same kind of system, however, may well work in selling commodity items, especially if home delivery is included in the deal. Telaction was simply ahead of its time. By 2000, Americans will be ready to buy via television.

This doesn't mean that shopping malls will become deserted. It does mean that they will not see the sales increases that were registered over the past three decades. It also might mean that some malls will go out of business. Those who would be discomfitted the most by this little trend will be those lovingly called "mall rats" by retailers. They are the senior citizens, the unemployed mothers and the teenagers. For some of the kids going to the mall is a way of life. They spent a good deal of their childhoods trailing their mothers through the shopping center or hanging out at the mall's Burger King. Someday during the next decade this young generation may well discover a revolutionary new kind of retail establishment, a freestanding store on a downtown city street.

FUTURE SCOPE

———————— ADVISORY ————————

Trends

- Despite the increase in sex education, the number of out-of-wedlock births has quadrupled in the past 30 years, especially among women over 20.

- The number of single-person households and unmarried couples living together has grown rapidly. A majority of young couples live together before getting married.

- The size of the average American family is the smallest ever and is still declining. Boomers are in their peak family-forming years, which should enhance family values in the 1990s.

- Americans have turned into grazers as more meals are eaten away from home or purchased from carryout stores.

- Shopping patterns have changed, with consumers making more short trips to supermarkets.

Strategies

- Employers should establish home-based work forces to cut expenses and accommodate women who want to work and raise children.

- Developers should consider smaller housing units in the next decade for smaller families and single-person households.

- The growth of huge hypermarkets will increase the need for smaller, quick-stop convenience stores. Stores should prepare for an increase in two-income families with less time to shop.

- The market for meals away from home and carryout food will expand rapidly in the coming decade.

PART 2

MAKING A LIVING
IN THE 1990s

CHAPTER 6

The Shrinking Middle Class

The old saying about the rich getting richer and the poor getting poorer isn't merely a saying. That is exactly what has happened in the United States over the past 20 years. While the gap is widening between the richest and the poorest of our society, demographers say the middle class is actually shrinking as a percentage of our population. By 1988, affluent households, those described as having incomes of $50,000 or more a year, had grown to include about one-fourth of the nation's households. (Some analysts use different income levels. We decided on $50,000 because it is so widely used.) Even when adjusted for inflation, this category had nearly doubled in percentage since 1970. This group earns half of the country's income and controls two-thirds of its discretionary dollars. Using the same constant dollars, the share of households earning $15,000 to $50,000 declined from about 59% in 1970 to about 53% in 1988. The percentage of households with incomes of less than $15,000 increased slightly to about 22%.

If the trend continues it will turn us into an increasingly polarized nation by the end of the 1990s. Not that the vast difference between the very rich and the very poor isn't evident today. All one has to do is visit New York City to see the two economic worlds orbiting in surrealistically close juxtaposition. This is a city with more than its share of high-powered, highly paid investment bankers, advertising executives and media stars. They live in a world of six- or seven-figure salaries, $100 lunch tabs and Fire Island weekends. But when they step out of their gleaming office buildings to hurry to their waiting limousines, they pass within feet of people who have no money, no homes and live off scraps and charity. When the well-groomed executives stride through the corridors of Grand Central Station, escaping the stress of the city on the way to their $800,000 suburban homes, they walk through a gauntlet of shabby homeless seeking refuge from the cold night air.

But New York doesn't have all of the country's homeless. This growing underclass has spread to most corners of the United States, but mainly big cities like Chicago, Los Angeles and San Francisco. Homeless can also be found in smaller cities like Portland, Oregon and suburbs like Evanston, Illinois. These homeless, the poorest of the poor, are only the visual symbols of our polarized society. The great majority of the poor are invisible to the affluent sector of our society. But even if we can't see them, they can be found in the statistics that come rolling out of the U.S. Census Bureau. These statistics say that the percentage of Americans living below the poverty level has not changed substantially in 20 years. About 14% of Americans exist on subpoverty incomes, representing about 35 million persons. Among children, the numbers are even worse. About 20% of the nation's children live in poverty. That situation exists because the poor are more likely to have children than the rich, and they tend to have more children.

The percentage of children living in poverty has increased significantly in the past 20 years. Back in 1970, less than 15% lived below the poverty level. While the increase is only five percentage points, it represents a 33% increase over the 1970 total. What might be surprising to most readers is that the percentage of black children living in poverty has remained fairly static while large increases have been registered by white and Hispanic children. Much of this is due to the increase in single-parent households, especially when the parent is a woman. Because of the child-caring burden, the woman often must take a lower-paying job close to her home. Or she may be forced to settle for a part-time job at a minimal pay level.

The increase in poor children, however, has been more than matched by a decrease in poor senior citizens. Twenty years ago, about 25% of those 65 and over lived below the poverty level, compared with about 12% today. This is primarily a result of improvements in Social Security, Medicare and private pension plans. But maybe the biggest reason for the difference in trends for youngsters and oldsters is that the senior citizens can vote. Children aren't a very influential lobbying group.

Losing the War on Poverty

The most distressing fact for Americans to contemplate is that we have not been able to do anything to reduce the poor population. No matter what social programs have been put into place or which ones scrapped, the numbers have remained fairly constant. Even the prolonged economic recovery and expansion after the 1982 recession didn't put a dent in our poverty levels. The only thing we did was to trade in poor old people in exchange for poor young people. If nothing else it proved that the Social Security system works.

There is a glimmer of hope for the poor in the decade to come, but only a glimmer. The oncoming shortage of labor might help open up some jobs for the poor and unemployed. The jobs that open up will be on the low end of the economic scale but may be able to provide a second income in many families, which might push total earnings over the poverty level. In fact, one reason for the movement of so many families into the over-$50,000 bracket is the increase in two-income households. Similarly, a good portion of those who dropped from the middle-income group into the subpoverty group were those single-parent households we mentioned earlier. These are households with no chance of adding a second salary to family income.

The overall outlook for the poor and the lower middle class is bleak. There is nothing on the horizon that will help pull any significant percentage of them up into the middle-income ranks. Fifty years ago many high-salaried manufacturing jobs provided those with high school educations or less a good income. The number of those jobs is shrinking. Young people who go into the work force in the 1990s with only a high school education will have fewer high-paying career opportunities than their parents did. The jobs that our economy will create for these people in the next decade are virtually all in the service sector, where salaries are lower than in manufacturing. The social strata of the next decade will be based almost totally on education.

While the uneducated lower middle class remains mired in a world of diminishing opportunities, the middle class will continue to shrink. That is because more middle-class Americans are getting higher educations and pushing their way into the affluent ranks. In previous generations they would have been white-collar workers. Now they are going on to college and filling the ever-growing demand for professionals, managers and technical specialists.

All of this means, of course, that the gap between rich and poor will continue to widen, creating some ominous overtones for the twenty-first century. One point to remember is that most of those living in poverty aren't unemployed. They are working but not earning enough money to afford life's necessities, not to mention luxuries. They are called the "working poor."

Looking at the concurrent trends in place, there is little chance that very many of these working poor will be able to free themselves from their economic traps. The cost of housing, medical care and a college education is rising far more rapidly than their incomes. They are not catching up; they are falling behind.

A Lower Standard of Living

That observation may also be true for all of America. It is almost certain that our standard of living, when compared with the rest of the world, will at best be static in the next decade. But it most likely will decline somewhat. Most other industrialized countries are growing more rapidly than we are, especially two of our Far East trading partners, Japan and South Korea. Third World countries, fed by the influx of manufacturing in the past two decades, are also outpacing us. The devaluation of the dollar in the late 1980s gave ample evidence that our standard of living, which had been climbing for many years, had paused for a rest. We were paying more dollars for imports but getting fewer yens, marks, pounds and francs for our exports.

While the cost of imported goods was going up at 20% a year, our salaries were climbing by only 5%. All of a sudden consumers realized that the price of that cute little Japanese car they were considering had crept up to $22,000.

Americans who traveled to Europe in the late 1980s found that for the first time hotel rooms in Rome, Paris and London were more expensive than in New York. While Tokyo has always been more expensive than the United States, the $100-plus cab ride from the airport to a downtown hotel is still an eye-opener. If you want to meet foreigners, the best way is to stay right here in the United States because more of them are going to visit here than ever before. The devaluation of the dollar has made this country a vacation bargain, especially for those who live in other industrialized countries of the world, such as Japan and West Germany.

There is no simple way to deal with the concept of standard of living. It is a term that is used loosely — which is appropriate because there is no universally accepted definition or method of measuring the level of basic necessities and luxuries that we can afford. Making more money doesn't mean one can afford to buy more. Many blue-blooded families found that their standard of living slipped in the early part of this century when it became difficult to hire live-in servants. Young people rebelled against those feudal-like relationships in favor of factory jobs where they could get more money and freedom at the same time.

We have all seen little bites taken out of our standards of living. We pump our own gas these days. We try on shoes and clothes unassisted at the discount store. We buy "wood" furniture but find that it is made of compressed sawdust. We talk to answering machines instead of secretaries. We buy dress shirts with average-length sleeves rather than exact-length sleeves.

Most economists contend that productivity is the key to a higher standard of living for all of us. If companies can derive more income for each man-hour of work, they will pay higher wages to their employees. It is this kind of accelerating productivity that has sparked advances in so many other industrialized and Third World countries. And it is precisely where the United States has lagged in recent years. Measured in constant dollars, median household income has shown virtually no increase in 20 years. For most of the 1950s and 1960s, the United States was experiencing productivity gains of more than 3% a year. By the mid-1980s, the rate was down to 1% a year. The higher productivity gains made in many foreign countries during the past decade explains why they have been able to attain living standards comparable to, or better than, ours.

Technological advancements in manufacturing lead directly to increases in productivity. But in the next decade the great majority of new jobs generated will be in the service sector, where it is more difficult to improve productivity than it is in the manufacturing sector. There are many ways in which to boost productivity in a factory assembly line but very few ways to improve the productivity of a barber or a classroom teacher.

As a result of the overwhelming movement toward service industry jobs, the prospect of a sharply higher productivity rate for the United States in the 1990s is very unlikely. We will continue to compromise on service and quality throughout the decade as we see our standard of living slip to a lower level.

Another Kind of "Homeless"

For generations the major fantasy of the American dream was to buy one's own home. In a study conducted a couple of years ago, Americans were asked to name the important components of the good life. The biggest single response, 87%, mentioned owning a home, compared with 80% who identified a happy marriage, 78% an interesting job, or 62% who chose having a lot of money. It didn't matter if the home was a suburban mansion, a stunning high-rise condominium or a modest cottage in the country. Home ownership symbolized stability and status. It still does. But many of those trying to live out the American dream are experiencing a rude awakening. In the 1980s, for the first time since the Great Depression, the percentage of Americans owning homes started to decline. In 1940, less than 44% of American families owned their homes. That share grew to 65% in 1980 but then started a slow slide to about 63% in the late 1980s.

Some economists felt at first that the early decline was nothing more than a slight hiccup in a gradual upward trend. But by the end of the 1980s it became clear that home ownership had peaked and something substantial would have to change in order for it to start rising again. Many of those who weren't concerned about the downward trend said that it was caused by other demographic changes. Couples were getting married later in life, they said, or they weren't getting married at all. That argument didn't prove out when it was shown that the percentage of homes bought by single persons and unmarried persons living together is continuing to increase.

In 1983, 85% of all first-time home buyers were married couples. This has since slipped to 70%. There is, of course, good reason for this trend. Single persons and unmarried couples usually have no children, which frees up more money to spend on housing. Looking down the road, we would project that the percentage of homes purchased by childless couples and individuals will continue to increase. That will be a function of families having fewer children and a growing number having no children.

The Middle Class Is Hurt Most

The major decrease in home ownership has taken place among traditional middle-class families earning $30,000 to $60,000 a year, with first-time home buyers hit especially hard. They simply weren't able to amass the down payment necessary for a home and still obtain enough credit to carry a large mortgage. What happened was that they were being attacked on two fronts. The major obstacle was the rapid escalation in housing prices, which in some areas were increasing by as much as 20% a year. The median price of a new single-family home in the United States soared from about $23,000 in 1970 to more than $100,000 by 1988. Median income tripled in that period, but the cost of housing more than quadrupled.

But that was only part of the problem. Home prices were escalating even more rapidly in areas where local economies were creating jobs at a high rate. By the late 1980s, the disparity in median home prices across the country was greater than it had ever been. The median home price in Chicago, for example, was about $100,000; on the West Coast and in the Northeast, concurrent medians were running from $175,000 to $200,000.

One survey conducted by Coldwell Banker, the real estate firm, indicated that a typical four-bedroom, 2½-bath home with a two-car garage would sell for $150,000 to $250,000 in the Chicago area; but the same house would range from $500,000 to $700,000 in

Washington, D.C. and from $900,000 to $1,500,000 in Santa Monica, California.

Even as we approach 1990, the disparity continues to grow. The average value of a home in San Francisco increased by 32% in 1988. In Los Angeles the increase was 31%.

The second area of attack on home buyers came from high interest rates, which soared during the superinflation of the late 1970s. Mortgage rates subsided somewhat in the next decade but never went down to the "normal" levels of 6% to 8% that welcomed home buyers in the 1960s.

There is no way to predict where interest rates are headed in the next decade, but there are a couple of indicators that may signal whether rates will advance or decline. Many economists say that the interest rates will not decline significantly until the federal budget deficit is trimmed. By the end of the 1980s there was little consensus that this would happen. Another factor affecting interest rates is inflation — high inflation generates high interest rates. This indicator was running slightly above normal rates in the late 1980s but considerably less than a decade earlier. The conservative prediction would indicate that mortgage rates will probably remain in the historically high range of 8.5% to 12% throughout most of the 1990s.

The Housing Budget Goes Up

Among the various categories of families, those who were experiencing the greatest difficulty in attaining their dream home were first-time home buyers, who tend to be younger. Before 1975 this group helped fuel the demand for housing as they accounted for 45% of all house sales. Ten years later, first-timers were accounting for only 35% of purchases.

Among the lucky Americans who were able to buy their first homes, a new trend was emerging: They were spending a greater percentage of their incomes on shelter than any previous generation. The rule of thumb applied during the post–World War II building boom advised first-time home buyers to spend no more than 25% of their incomes on shelter. For more than 25 years, expenditures on shelter (which includes mortgage, insurance and utilities) did run in that range for the average first-time home buyer. But when home prices soared and interest rates soared even higher in the late 1970s, the percentage of income new buyers were spending on their homes had climbed to more than 38%. That percentage declined in the 1980s but was still running at more than 30% at the end of the decade.

Another reason that made it more difficult for young families to buy homes was the demand by lenders for larger down payments. First-timers had traditionally come up with the equivalent of one-third of their annual income as down payment on their first homes. But by the late 1980s the average down payment equaled half of their annual incomes. The average American family could no longer afford the average American home.

How then, you might ask, was anybody able to break into the housing market in the past decade? The prime reason goes back to another major trend that has been building: a larger percentage of women and mothers going into the work force. It has been the increase in two-income households that has given first-timers the leverage to buy homes. In fact, among first-time home buyers, as many as 85% are two-income households.

One interesting theory forwarded by critics is that many young buyers—especially those we have come to know and love as Yuppies—are overextending themselves on housing because they have set their sights too high. The earlier generation bought their first homes in modest or even run-down city neighborhoods, then worked their way up to bigger homes in the suburbs. Many of today's young couples spent the early years of their marriages (or "relationships," if you please) enjoying themselves. They lived in trendy high-priced rental apartments, bought fancy imported cars, wore designer clothes, went on idyllic vacations, dined out five times a week and then one day decided they wanted to move into a suburban dream home. The prices they encountered and the down payments required gave them a healthy case of sticker shock. Aside from participating in the American dream by owning their homes, young people have another motivation for buying: The home they acquire will be a major investment, and they will be looking for a return on their investment in a few years. Sure, Americans have always looked at their homes as an investment, but this ideal didn't turn into real dollars until housing prices started climbing steeply in the 1970s.

Today's young buyers have heard stories of an earlier generation of families – perhaps even their parents – who bought modest suburban homes for $20,000 and sold them 20 years later for $200,000. Prospective buyers in their 20s have learned that home ownership can have its economic rewards as well as its psychic rewards. Whether it is wise or not, many young families are spending to the limit to buy their first home.

Financial planners would probably advise against putting so much of the family's income and resources into the family home. On the other hand, most financial experts believe that buying a home is the most basic and usually the best investment anyone can make.

The main problem, however, is that so many buyers think they are going to make a killing when they decide to sell their homes a couple of years down the line. Although home prices have increased dramatically in recent years, there is no guarantee that they will continue to increase in the future. What they fail to realize is that in the first half of this century, median home prices were static for periods of a decade or more; in some spans prices even declined. As you will see later in this chapter, there is a real possibility of that happening again.

A Lack of Saving Grace

If Americans are spending so much more of their incomes on housing, where is this money coming from? By all indications it appears that we have shifted funds from our savings into housing. Indeed, for many of those described above, buying a house has become their primary method of saving. They are obliged to make the mortgage payment every month, which forces them to save.

That sounds good, but it isn't totally logical. Anyone who has bought a home knows that in the early years of a mortgage virtually all of the payment goes for interest and only a pittance for principal. It is only in these relatively recent years of rapid price appreciation that buyers have been able to build up equity in their homes in such a short time. And that isn't the same as saving, which, based on the old-fashioned definition, is nothing more than spending less money than you make.

Going back 40 years, Americans traditionally saved 7% to 9% of their disposable personal income. This figure started plummeting in the late 1970s and by 1987 had hit a low of 3.2%. The rate rebounded to 4.2% in 1988 but was still a far cry from the 10% to 20% savings rates usually racked up in Japan and many European countries.

One figure that shows the importance of home owning to Americans is their net worth. Homes account for more than 41% of the total net worth of Americans. Compare this with all of their savings in interest-bearing accounts and funds, which is only 18% of their net worth. Many experts feel that those who are most at risk during this savings drain are the Baby Boomers. When they start retiring in 20 years their life expectancy will be much longer than those retiring today. That is a very pleasant outlook, of course, but only if the retiree has provided for enough funds to carry him or her through those extra years.

The downside of extended longevity is that much of it will be accomplished through more advanced medical treatment and procedures. The cost of health care has escalated more than any other important category of spending in the past 40 years, from less than 5% of all American spending in 1955 to more than 12% by 1985. And the elderly need more health care than any other age group. Even in recent years, with public and private cost-containment programs such as health maintenance organizations and preventive medicine, the cost of health care has risen more rapidly than the inflation rate. It would be foolish to project at this point that health care costs will start to increase at a slower rate. The Baby Boomers will have to pay for living those extra years—or at least someone will pay for them. Within the next few years we undoubtedly will see federal legislation aimed at curtailing health care costs or providing umbrella coverage for major illnesses.

The prospect of some kind of national health care plan has been discussed for years in the United States. These discussions will heat up even more as medical costs continue to rise. We predict that there will be no slackening of these rises until the medical profession itself leads a serious effort at cost containment. Because a health insurance plan or catastrophic illness plan is a federal program doesn't mean it will be free. All it means is that the cost of the program will be spread out across a wider range of taxpayers.

No matter what happens, the cost of health care and related topics may well turn into the most-discussed social issue of the next ten years. Various kinds of insurance will be available, but if current trends persist these forms of insurance will pay for a decreasing share of medical costs. Substantial saving will be absolutely necessary in the coming years if retired persons expect to stay off the welfare rolls.

Caring for Old Boomers

Even if the physical health care issue is resolved, retiring Baby Boomers will have another problem brought on by their longevity: They will require greater long-term care in retirement homes or geriatric centers. This usually is not covered by Medicare or private insurance plans but generally has been paid for directly by families. With Americans living longer and being more physically fit, we might also expect that they will have longer periods of senility and other mental problems of the aged, necessitating more personal care for them.

Early in this century the younger generation took on the responsibility of caring for the elderly. Families were far more important then. They usually lived closer together, in the same town or even on the same block. When Grandmother was widowed she usually would move into the home of her children and grandchildren, becoming part of the immediate family again. She helped with the cooking and with caring for the kids. If Grandma got sick the family cared for her. There wasn't all that much need for Social Security, pensions, IRAs and Medicare. And Grandma never needed to have much in savings because her family was always there.

With the splintering of American families today, that situation has turned into a nostalgic fantasy. When most Baby Boomers reach retirement age, moving in with their children won't even be an alternative. One reason is mobility. The kids will probably live halfway across the country maybe because the son-in-law accepted a job offer on the other coast, or maybe because Grandma and Grandpa moved to the Sunbelt after they retired. That will make it less likely for them to move back into the family circle.

Another reason is divorce, which has increased dramatically in the past four decades. The relationship that has suffered the most in divorces is that between fathers and children. Researchers say that more than half of divorced fathers never or rarely see their children. When these fathers grow old and need care it is almost certain that they will not move in with their children. In addition, their estranged children will probably feel no responsibility to contribute financial support.

Even if families are whole, however, and the relationships are healthy, there will be another obstacle to a disabled grandparent moving in with the family. Where will the daughter or daughter-in-law be who used to provide this care? In the old days she was home. In 2000 and beyond, she most likely will be at work. Her child, if she has one, will be at a day-care center. Don't expect her to give up her job and stay home to take care of Grandma.

Because of all of these trends developing at the same time, it becomes clear that Baby Boomers will have to rely more on savings than previous generations have. Unfortunately, they appear to be saving less. The greatest disappointment might well be felt by those who have made their family home the keystone of their savings program. They feel that when they reach retirement age they will sell their home and come away with a nice nest egg. We cannot predict housing prices ten or 20 years into the future, but we can use some common sense in projecting what the trends will be. And the trends are working against the Baby Boomers. After all, they came into the work force along with a major surge of people, so salaries were relatively modest. The Baby Busters will do better on the average because there are fewer of them to fill job vacancies.

Baby Boomers also went into the housing market en masse and were part of the reason that prices escalated so rapidly. But all indications are that the demand for housing will decline in the early years of the twenty-first century because there are fewer Baby Busters who will be starting families. With the big supply of Baby Boomer homes and the small demand by Baby Busters, chances are that home prices will moderate or may drop in the next 20 years.

That should be enough ominous warnings for Baby Boomers, but there is yet another. Regardless of what politicians promise, no one can guarantee that Social Security will continue to upgrade the economic level of retired people. While the Social Security system started to build up a surplus in the 1980s to compensate for the bulge of Baby Boom retirees, that surplus has been used to offset some of the huge federal budget deficits racked up in the decade. In other words, the surplus is only a government accounting entry. The formula to keep the Social Security system viable was based on government assumptions of an almost-perfect set of economic circumstances for the next 20 years: low inflation, solid economic growth, no recessions. In other words, a highly unlikely scenario. By 2010, when the Baby Boomers start to retire, there really may be no surplus at all. People who retire in the next century will be receiving their Social Security benefits largely from the workers paying into the system at the time.

Economic Challenge of the 1990s

Much of this chapter could be described as a dire prediction for the future, but this is not an exercise in doomsaying. We aren't at the doorstep of a national economic disaster. Anyone expecting to live into the twenty-first century, however, should realize that economic progress is not a constitutional right. Among many segments of American culture it has been important that generations move up, so that the next generation has more and enjoys more than the past generation. With the trends that are in place, it will become increasingly difficult for families to mark this kind of economic progress.

One important advantage that will help most Americans cope with the problems of the next decade is their growing financial sophistication. The vast majority of people in this country have a better notion of personal finance than any other previous generation. And they learned the hard way, through the bitter lessons of experience. Those brought up during the depression years learned some elementary lessons in how the vagaries of the world economy could affect their own microeconomic circumstances. But that generation didn't have the educational background of today's Americans. By the 1970s, when the OPEC nations doubled the price of petroleum almost overnight, Americans learned how world oil prices would affect the cost of operating their personal cars. They responded by using less gasoline — either driving less or switching to more fuel-efficient cars. Inflation taught them another vivid lesson in personal economics. So did high interest rates and the declining value of the dollar. The stock market crash of October 19, 1987, provided another lesson. As a result of all of this practical education—added to their academic education—Americans today have become conversant with such macroeconomic topics as the national debt, the price of gold, the foreign trade deficit, and the relative values of the world's currencies.

This is a valuable, indeed a necessary, education for grappling with the ever-growing complexities that the economy of the next decade will generate.

FUTURE SCOPE

─────── *A*DVISORY ───────

Trends

- The gap between America's poorest and most affluent is widening, and the size of the middle class is shrinking.

- More children are living under the poverty level, while the percentage of poor senior citizens is declining.

- The American standard of living will slip in the 1990s as other industrialized countries catch up with us.

- The percentage of home-owning families is shrinking, and first-time buyers are having trouble meeting the sharply higher home prices.

- We are spending far more on shelter but putting far less into savings.

- Because of increased longevity and soaring health costs, Boomers may face economic problems when they retire in the twenty-first century.

Strategies

- Government agencies may have to consider some kind of Social Security for youngsters as well as retirees.

- Companies will have to strive for higher productivity in order to enhance the standard of living.

- Public or private agencies should study the financial needs of young families that can't afford to buy housing.

- Boomers will have to save more and plan in advance for retirement incomes in case Social Security flops.

CHAPTER 7

Women's Equality Is in Sight

The women's movement crept into existence about 25 years ago, prompting scorn and derision from many circles. But long after the revolutionary bombastics of bra burning and picketing flickered out, an evolution has continued. Even though the economic and political progress made by women has seemed agonizingly slow for some, the progress has been real and has come steadily. Based on several trends already in movement, a far more substantial payoff for women will come in the next decade.

By 2000 women will truly have achieved equality of opportunity in the workplace. But don't jump to conclusions. These words have been chosen carefully so as not to intimate that women's political and economic power will match that of men within the next decade. That kind of equality will take many more decades, if indeed it ever comes about.

By 2000 men will still dominate the nation's business sector. The difference between then and now will be that women will have made dramatic inroads. We predict that a half-dozen or more Fortune 500 corporations will be headed by women. At the same time, a half-dozen U.S. senators will be women, as will 75 or more members of the House of Representatives. There are two major reasons why this progress will occur. The first is that a significant number of women born in the 1960s and 1970s have different goals from those born 20 years earlier. That alone would be enough to signal the future change that will inevitably come. But another factor has crept into our social attitudes, one that accepts women in nontraditional roles, even in the role of business, political or thought leader. This attitude certainly isn't held universally yet, but it gradually is taking hold. The blind resistance to the idea of women as equals—which predominated in the 1960s—has worn down considerably.

The Equal Rights Amendment to the U.S. Constitution, defeated after a long and bitter fight several years ago, was an idea ahead of its time. It would probably be approved today even though a sizable number of Americans still actively or passively oppose equality for women and want them to remain in their pre-1960s traditional roles. This group tends to be made up of males who are less educated and less affluent, and of females who want to live their lives traditionally and would just as soon see all other women do the same thing. By and large, most opponents of women's equality are those who do not have a lot of personal power and feel threatened by someone else acquiring power.

The progress we predict for women over the next decade isn't mere speculation but rather a projection of the evolution that has been taking place over the past 30 years. There is no indication that the evolution will be reversed. We see no backlashes or reassertions of male domination. In fact, the evolution toward more power for women will probably accelerate in the last half of the 1990s.

There is no single measurement by which to calculate how women have amassed a greater share of power in recent years, but let's look at some of the indicators. Congress is one example. In 1971, there were 12 women in the House of Representatives. By 1989, there were 25. That represents a significant increase in less than 20 years. We predict that the increase will be even larger in the next decade.

Where do congressmen (or women) come from? Most often they move up through the political ranks, the most important stop being in their state legislatures. These state legislatures are the minor leagues, so to speak, to the major league of Congress. And there have never been more women in the minor leagues than there are right now. Between 1975 and 1989, the number of women serving as state legislators doubled to about 1,200, and the number of women serving on county boards tripled to more than 1,500. By the end of the 1990s, as many as 35% to 40% of the nation's state legislators will probably be women.

When talking about politics the question that usually comes up is whether we will have a woman president by 2000. Obviously, no one can answer that with any certainty. In 1984 Geraldine Ferraro became the first woman to run for vice president on a major party ticket. Although she and presidential candidate Walter Mondale lost the election, it wasn't because of her gender. Ferraro's nomination didn't raise as many eyebrows as Dan Quayle's vice presidential nomination did four years later. This was a milestone because it signified that at least one major political party was ready to accept a woman vice president — which means, in effect, they also were ready to accept a woman president. Even in defeat, the Mondale-Ferraro ticket attracted 37.5 million votes from the public. This substantial number of votes, along with the fact that more women are being elected to public office, shows clearly that gender will not be as important an issue in the political arena of the next decade as it was in preceding decades.

Along with the growing acceptance of women as leaders, it also has become obvious that the pool of women qualified for high position is growing. This is the case not only with politics but also business and the professions. There is no single reason why women finally seem to be headed on the path to power. As you will see in the paragraphs to come, many factors have contributed to an environment that has allowed women to choose alternatives to the traditional female role in our society. Of course, there is a substantial portion of women who still follow the traditional, but that portion has declined steadily over the past 20 years and will continue to decline.

Let's consider some of the key transitions in the changing female landscape and see how they influence each other. In an earlier chapter, for example, we saw how the median age at which women are getting married has gradually advanced, from about 20 in the 1950s to nearly 24 in 1989. This is happening because of many profound transitions in our society. Women do not have as much parental and peer pressure to marry early, as they once did. In most sectors of American society during the first half of this century, young women lived with their parents until they got married. The lucky ones finished high school, got a clerical job and started looking for a husband. Women who had the support of their families went to college and

95

for the most part became teachers or nurses. Only a small fraction went into other professions. Many got married in college while others started looking for husbands as soon as they went into the work force.

But most women weren't lucky enough to go to college. As recently as 1960, more than 57% of adult women in the United States had not even completed four years of high school; that is an astounding statistic. When they were old enough to work, those girls got jobs as seamstresses, assembly line or laundry workers. Because they couldn't afford to go out on their own they lived at home and contributed money to their family's income while they looked for husbands to save them from their dreary lives. In some cultures, the only way many women could escape the domination of their parents was through marriage. Getting married at an early age was the most effective way for them to achieve freedom – not that the parents objected. Mom and Dad wanted them to marry early so they could get them out of the house and start looking forward to being grandparents. That whole lifestyle obviously has changed for most women. An increasing number of women, as well as men, move out of their family homes after school and set up their own households, either singly or with someone else.

Today's educated young women also aren't relegated to the former "pink-collar" ghetto of female jobs, such as secretary, teacher, nurse. They can aspire to professions of greater status and incomes – accountant, lawyer or architect, for example. What this reflects is another key factor: More women are going to college. This is another reason contributing to the fact that women are getting married later in life. To illustrate the dramatic increase in college-bound women, look at the difference in a recent 15-year span. Between 1970 and 1985, the number of women attending college increased by 82% while the number of male students increased by only 15%. In 1970 women made up 40% of all college students. As of the mid-1980s, for the first time in history more women than men were attending colleges and universities. If the trend continues, women will outnumber male college students substantially in the years to come and receive more college degrees.

Projecting this trend even further into the future, it means that more women than men will be qualified for jobs requiring higher educational levels and probably paying higher incomes. This is one of the factors that leads us to predict great strides by women over the next decade. It is altogether possible to sketch out a scenario for the next 50 years in which women not only match men in the world of work but actually surpass them. But we'll go no further with that notion except to point out the possibility of it coming about. We must note, however, the impact that women are having on some specific professions that previously were exclusive male enclaves. Of all accountants and auditors, 45% are women; of computer programmers, 40%; of lawyers, 15% (but that is up from only 10% in 1979, and women account for 30% of all new law degrees). Even in electrical engineering, long considered a male domain, the number of jobs held by women has increased from 4% to 9% in the past decade.

A 20-year comparison provided by the U.S. Department of Education illustrates the dramatic influx of women into previously men-only fields. The following figures show the college degrees conferred to women in some selected fields of study:

Field	1966	1976	1986
Business, Management, Accounting	5,263	28,112	108,889
Law	470	6,208	13,970
Engineering	143	1,460	12,581
Medicine	503	2,174	4,916
Computer Science	324 (1971)	1,118	14,966

This is strong evidence that women are approaching equality with men even in these traditional fields. They may never achieve real equality, but the trend still indicates that they are moving in that direction.

Narrowing the Pay Gap

Even though they have moved into what used to be typically male professions and trades, women still earn less than men on the average. But the gap is narrowing. Based on the average of all full-time workers, women make about 65 cents for every dollar earned by men. A decade earlier, women earned only 59 cents for every dollar earned by men. The comparison is even closer for women in their 20s, who are more likely to be college-educated than those in older age cohorts. They make about 80% of what men do. We expect that by 2000, the average earnings of all full-time women employees will be 75% to 80% of men's earnings.

But not all women are being outearned by men today. The U.S. Census Bureau estimates that more than five million working wives bring home more money than their husbands do. This accounts for more than 20% of all married couples in which both parties work. These women were more likely to have no minor children at home, to have completed college and to work in professional specialty occupations or executive, administrative and managerial positions. The flow of women into the work force is happening not only on the professional level but at all levels of employment. In 1960, women made up 33% of the work force. By 1986, they accounted for 45%. A study by the Conference Board showed that women comprised about two-thirds of all growth in the labor force during the 1980s. That same situation should extend throughout the 1990s as a growing percentage of women enter the job market. In 1970, 43% of the women 16 and older were in the labor force, compared with 80% of the men. By 1980, 52% of the women were working, compared with 77% of the men. The Bureau of Labor Statistics estimates that by 2000, nearly 62% of the women will be working, compared with 75% of the men. As you can see, women and men are going in opposite directions as far as work trends are concerned. It will be only a matter of time until there are more women than men in the work force. This probably will not happen, however, within the next decade.

The increased flow of women into the labor force is a function of several changes, but perhaps the most important one is a profound shift in the American lifestyle. It was once a rarity for the mother of small children to hold a job outside the home. In 1950, only 12% of women with children under six were in the labor force. Today, a mother who does not have a job outside the home is the exception, not the rule. As recently as 1976, only 31% of the women who had had babies in the previous 12 months were either working or actively looking for work. By 1987, this had shot up to 51%. Among all mothers with children under 18, 65% are in the labor force.

What we have here are Baby Boomers at work, women who finished high school and maybe even college. They took jobs after completing their educations and delayed getting married. When they finally did get married they delayed having their first child while they pursued their careers; or they simply lived out the stereotypical Yuppie lifestyle, enjoying the luxuries provided by two incomes and no children. Now after having that first child, the modern American woman heads back to work as soon as possible. A generation earlier, she probably would have stayed at home and become the "typical housewife." But a generation earlier the woman was far less likely to have obtained a college degree and probably didn't have a high school diploma. Some women still follow the old tradition, but their numbers are shrinking. And they will continue to shrink. Fewer than 10% of the households in the United States can be described as what used to be the typical family with two parents, the father working and the mother at home taking care of the children. In other words, what we might imagine as the typical family isn't typical at all; it's atypical.

Demographics show that mothers with college degrees are twice as likely to go into the work force as those who don't have a high school diploma. Because the number of women with college degrees is rising rapidly, we can project that the percentage of mothers returning to the work force also will rise. By 2000, as many as 70% of new mothers will return to work within a year of having their first child. Economics will have a lot to do with their decision to go back to work. As we have pointed out in an earlier chapter, the 1990s will be marked by a sharp decline in the number of entry-level job seekers. As a result, the shortage of workers will reach record proportions by the middle of the 1990s. This will help push up wages, giving young mothers a solid incentive to get back into the job market.

There is no doubt that the lure of income is a major reason for the spurt in working mothers. The modern mother, with a higher educational level, is worth more on the job market than the previous generation of women who didn't even finish high school. Money isn't the only incentive, of course. Millions of women have expressed the need for self-fulfillment and self-worth. They don't want to feel totally dependent on their husbands, and they don't want to feel restricted to participating in the outside interests of other family members. They want lives of their own, apart from the family.

One additional factor that will contribute to the continued growth of women in the work force is the vast majority of jobs that will be created in the next decade in the service sector: white-collar, technical, retail, professional and managerial. These are occupations that women can handle as well as men. That is, no one can say women aren't strong enough or tall enough to be an accountant, for example. Over the next decade there will be virtually no growth in the typical blue-collar manufacturing jobs from which women were barred or discouraged for physical reasons. Another hurdle that service jobs have eliminated are the old-fashioned unions that discouraged newcomers—women or ethnic minorities—from entering trades. Most of the service occupations are nonunion.

This transition of women into power will produce not only monetary rewards for the female jobholder but also the psychic reward of self-fulfillment. In the twenty-first century, motherhood will not be the full-time job that it was for so many millions of American women in earlier generations. Childbirth will be merely a minor intermission in her career. Under this new order she will be able to raise a child—probably only one child—while still enjoying the personal satisfaction and income of a rewarding career.

One aspect of working motherhood that appears to be resolved is the question of maternal leaves of absence. Virtually all larger employers grant a disability leave of six to eight weeks and extend job protection to the mother. A majority of them also offer an additional unpaid leave of one to three months if the mother wants to spend additional time with her baby. In many cases the latter maternity benefit is also offered to men whose wives have had a baby.

When Work Isn't an Option

For some of those young mothers, going back to work will not be an option but a necessity. These mothers are single parents, their circumstances created by the doubling of the divorce rate in the past two decades. Divorce reached epidemic proportions in the 1970s, the first decade in which more marriages were ended by divorce than by death. Demographers estimate that about half of all marriages from the early 1970s will end in divorce.

The divorce rate, when measured as a percentage of population, apparently has plateaued in the past decade at about five divorces per 1,000 population. But we expect that a lot of publicity about divorce will be generated in the next decade because the ratio of divorces to marriages will rise dramatically. The reason: The dip in the number of teenagers in the 1980s will translate into a dip in the number of persons in their 20s, the most common age range for marriage. As a result, the number of marriages will decline in the 1990s while the number of divorces will continue to rise slowly.

Children of divorced parents, of course, overwhelmingly are placed in the custody of their mothers. Despite child support payments, divorced women who head households are usually forced to work.

Divorce is not the only generator of single-parent households. There also is a growing number of single women having children without the formality of marriage. Most of these single mothers fall into the lower income brackets and are obliged to seek work, apply for welfare, or both.

The Child Care Crunch

As this working-mother scenario expands in the next decade the demand for reliable quality child care will become crucial. Child care is destined to develop into a major challenge for industry and government, as well as for parents, in the 1990s. It also will evolve into a political football, perhaps on both the federal and local levels. Child care will be to the 1990s what Social Security was to the 1930s. There is no way to predict right now how the political winds will blow on this question, but the winds are sure to reach hurricane force.

Many industries already offer child care programs, realizing that this will be an employee benefit that might attract workers in the labor-shortage economy of the 1990s. Employer motivation is obvious. Child care can create a better worker—it can reduce tardiness and absenteeism and raise productivity and employee morale. A massive study conducted by the Bureau of Labor Statistics in 1987 indicated that only 2% of employers were providing company-sponsored day care for children of employees, and another 3% were providing financial assistance to help pay the cost of child care. The study was made of more than 1.2 million companies with ten or more employees. It showed that the larger a company is, the more likely it is to offer some kind of child care benefit. By 2000, however, child care will become a routine part of the employee benefit package.

101

Company-provided child care will take various forms. Some employers will provide child care facilities on the premises. Although this necessitates the greatest commitment by the employer it also might produce the most efficient results. After all, the mother or father doesn't have to make an additional stop at a day care facility on the way to and from work. The parent also will be able to see the child during the lunch hour or other break time. Many employers will consider paying child care subsidies for workers or even underwrite the establishment of outside child care facilities that can serve their employees. No matter how this develops, the combination of working mothers and the labor shortage will transform child care into a major industry by the end of the 1990s, perhaps comparable with what happened to the nursing home business in the 1970s.

We expect that all forms of child care services will grow rapidly during the 1990s. But we see the greatest demand for franchised operations that offer insured services, standardized operations and certified personnel. There are opportunities in this area for companies with well-known brand names. These can be consumer products manufacturers, retailers or even magazine publishers aimed at householders. With two-income families, the cost of such services is less important than the degree of confidence and peace of mind generated with the parents.

Can Work Lead to Divorce?

In this complex maze of influences and relationships, we must consider another possibility for the 1990s. As we have mentioned, the higher divorce rate is forcing many single mothers to go into the work force. One point to consider is whether the opposite influence is also taking place—that more working women and mothers will tend to push up the divorce rate even faster. A paper prepared by Dr. Julia Heath, Memphis State University, showed that the more hours a married woman works the greater the probability of divorce. The indications are that women might hedge against an unstable marriage by working more. This makes her more independent and financially capable of going through a divorce.

In the same manner, women making above-average incomes may increase their probability of getting divorced. "Further, women who earn very high wages relative to other working women," Dr. Heath writes, "are likely to be in more male-dominated professions, increasing their opportunities for finding a mate preferable to their current spouse." Although this is only a theory, it may bear watching in the years to come. As we have pointed out, women are attending college in greater numbers; they are moving more readily into male-dominated professions; and they are making more money. If the divorce rate rises, this set of circumstances may be the reason.

The "Supermom" Syndrome

In describing our projections and predictions for the status of women over the next decade, we obviously are talking about more than mere economics. Even the fact that greater career opportunities will be offered to a major portion of the American public is of secondary importance. What must be realized by all is that we are describing profound changes that will occur in our society's customs and mores. Many people will criticize these changes as being anti-family and maybe even antisocial. We are making no judgment here that these transitions are good or bad but only that they are almost certain to come.

One thing women will have to grapple with is the "supermom" syndrome. Is it possible to be an efficient executive, a loving mother, a sexy bed partner, a gourmet cook and a responsible and active member of the PTA all at the same time? Probably not. Compromises will have to be made, and there probably will be different compromises for different people. Perhaps the most common compromise will occur in the work sector. An increasing number of employers are offering "flextime," flexible work hours that allow a working mother to adjust her hours to coordinate with other obligations, such as getting children ready for school. By the late 1980s more than 43% of all American employers were offering flextime, double the proportion that offered the benefit ten years earlier. We predict that by 2000, 80% of the companies in the United States will be offering flexible work hours to their employees.

Another alternative offered to working mothers is job sharing, where two employees working part-time shifts or alternate days perform the duties of one regular full-time employee. About 16% of employers offer job sharing, with a heavy concentration in the retail business, where it is easiest to administer.

In addition to flextime and job sharing, employers are making some jobs more convenient by allowing employees to work in their homes, linked to their offices by telephone, computer modem and fax machine. This obviously makes it easier for a woman to be supermom, but we see this being used mainly for clerical work and not professional careers. These work-at-home arrangements grew significantly in the 1980s and apparently will continue to grow in the 1990s, but probably not at the rapid rate that so many observers are predicting.

There was some evidence in the late 1980s that working mothers have not plunged into their careers without at least a twinge of conscience. A nationwide survey of more than 4,500 career women conducted by *Working Woman* magazine indicated that the transition is causing mixed emotions among many female executives. Nearly two-thirds of the working mothers said they buy fancy and expensive takeout food because of the hours they work. But half said they felt guilty serving prepared foods to their families instead of homecooked meals. More than 80% of the mothers with young children said they consciously try to recreate the warm family time around the dinner table that they remember from their childhoods.

Speaking of dinner, we must be sure to mention what has developed into the most valuable tool for working mothers: the microwave oven. Surveys indicate that a majority of working mothers use their microwave ovens nearly every day. The kitchen ranges of the 1990s would be better suited to the new women of the 1990s if they dropped those big ovens used for bread and pies and instead included speedy microwave ovens. The availability of the microwave has led to the marketing of a wide range of frozen dinners and other frozen foods that can be served to a hungry family after only a few minutes of microwave zapping. The selection and sales of these items will multiply in the next decade. A study of supermarket frozen food counters shows that the selection of products has already broadened into subcategories, such as gourmet foods, low-calorie entrées and larger portions for bigger appetites. Not only must the housewife/mother bring the food home, she must provide an interesting variety, perhaps her way of assuaging guilt by lavishing food on her children and husband (if there *is* a husband).

The working mother, as mentioned earlier, is also more likely to buy takeout foods on the way home from work, from fried chicken and barbecued ribs to pizza, Chinese food and whatever other fare becomes popular. The family with both parents or the single parent in the work force also is likely to eat out more often. This should continue the demand for moderately priced, family-oriented restaurants.

Daddy Does Dishes

One phenomenon that has come under considerable study is the reaction of fathers in families in which the mother is working. The studies generally show that the men are more likely to do some of the housework than was common in earlier times—but women shouldn't raise their hopes for more help. A study conducted by the University of Maryland showed that between 1965 and 1985, the average woman over 18 had decreased the amount of time spent on cooking, cleaning and laundry by eight hours a week. In that same span, the time spent by men on the same chores increased by two hours a week. But here's the kicker: As of 1985 the average woman was devoting 16 hours a week to the household chores, which was still four times as much as men. In interpreting the data we also must consider that the number of single men and divorced men living alone had increased steeply in that 20-year period. We can only assume that they are doing their own household chores.

Our prediction for the 1990s is that men will increase their household worktime very, very slowly. But don't look for a major trend to develop. Various surveys estimate that about 90% of married women who work full-time are also doing the family food shopping, cooking and laundry.

Because men often gauge the value of their household chores by how much they make per hour at work, we expect a vastly growing market for domestic services. Concurrent with the demand for child care we see the need for a "brand-name" or franchised network of domestic services that can take care of the home interior the way ChemLawn takes care of the grass.

Toward a Unisex World?

One of the topics that will become grist for the mill of social psychologists over the next decade will be the blurring of differences between the sexes. Some have said that the sexes are converging – women becoming more like men, men more like women. That is only half right. As we see it women are definitely moving into what used to be primarily male turf. They are attaining higher levels of education, getting better jobs, making more money. They are even smoking more and suffering more from stress.

But housework aside, we see very few, if any, areas in which men are acquiring female characteristics or emulating female mannerisms. Most men like the superior position that society has thrust upon them, and they don't have any desire to adopt the feminine role.

The masculinization of women is opening up many marketing opportunities for the business world. One of them is in the automobile business, which used to be dominated by men. Less than a decade ago women accounted for 36% of new car sales. Now they buy 48% of all new cars, and it's estimated they might move up to 60% by 2000. This trend should prompt changes in the way cars arc sold and serviced, although Detroit is renowned for its intransigence. Nevertheless, we expect to see more women selling cars on the showroom floors. Advertising already is starting to change, showing an increasing number of women behind the wheel. Whether that affects women's car-buying patterns is yet to be determined. Statistics show that women buy only 28% of Detroit's big cars, but they account for 55% of all subcompact and compact sales and 51% of imports. If women truly are becoming more like men, it will be interesting to see whether they become more likely to purchase full-size cars over the next ten years.

Working mothers and career women will create new demands on retail stores, food marketers and service providers of all kinds. Those who can anticipate the changing women's market and respond appropriately will look forward to a prosperous decade.

Trends

- Women will make dramatic strides toward equality in the 1990s, gaining economic and political power.

- Women are rejecting the old practice of getting married at an early age. Today they are more likely to go to college than men are.

- Young women are flooding into fields that formerly were closed to them, such as law, accounting and computer sciences. They also are narrowing the pay gap with men.

- The percentage of working mothers will grow through the next decade. One major reason is the increase in divorced women with children.

- The demand for child care will be a major social problem in the 1990s.

Strategies

- Corporations, institutions, professions and men will all have to adapt to the increase of women at top management levels.

- Government and employers will have to grapple with the challenge of providing child care in order to attract women to work.

- Employers will have to devise flexible working hours and shared jobs to accommodate working mothers.

- Opportunities will expand for those who can provide a variety of services to the legion of working mothers.

CHAPTER 8

A Nation of Nomads Keeps on Moving

For a time in the early 1980s it appeared that the American lust for relocation was starting to temper. Our hectic rate of moving from one place to another was showing evidence of a slowdown. In the 1960s more than 20% of all Americans on the average changed their addresses every year. By the 1970s this had slipped to 19%. In 1980–81, Census Bureau trackers found that only 17% of the U.S. population had changed its address. It appeared we were becoming more stable, less nomadic. Americans finally were settling down, an apparently developing trend being charted by demographers. Only one thing was wrong: Nothing of the kind was happening at all.

By the mid-1980s the quest for new digs had reawakened. Between March 1984 and March 1985, 46 million Americans moved from one house or apartment to another. This was up 18% from the previous year and marked the largest gain in mobility since the 1950s.

From our vantage point on the doorstep of the 1990s we project that the massive moving by Americans will not only continue but may even increase during the next decade. Looking back on the slowdown that occurred in the late 1970s and early 1980s, it appears that there was no slackening of our basic urge to pull up stakes and go somewhere else. What we saw was the impact of economics on the American lifestyle. The quadrupling of oil prices in the mid-1970s led to soaring inflation levels never before witnessed in this century.

This was accompanied by torrid interest rates, which caused the housing market to screech to a halt. Gasoline prices shot up to more than $1.50 a gallon, prompting Americans to drive less.

These factors influenced Americans to sit tight. How could a family think of buying a new house when the mortgage rates were rising almost daily? If they were sitting on a 6% mortgage in their current house they weren't likely to pony up 16% for a mortgage on a new house just because it has a nicer family room.

The high-interest period segued into the 1981–82 recession, which once again slowed down home sales. The unemployment rate approached 10% in 1982 and 1983, another dampening factor on the moving rate. As soon as the economy brightened, however, Americans went right back to their old habit of changing addresses at the slightest motivation.

Several factors playing out in the next decade will keep the moving rate high. The most important is that the economy is fundamentally sound. If we have a recession, it is projected to be short and mild. Inflation may be higher than it was in the late 1980s but nowhere near the double-digit level of the late 1970s. Interest rates will be above the historical average but still below the levels at which a majority of homeowners won't consider a move.

Another significant factor is that home ownership is lower today than it was in 1980. That means there are more renters, and renters are three times more likely to move than homeowners are. There also are more single-person and more nonfamily households, both of which are more conducive to a higher moving rate.

Census Bureau figures also show that college graduates move at a higher rate than those with a high school education or less. Because the number of college graduates is rising steadily, we expect that it will influence the moving rate to stay on the high side.

Despite all of these factors that give evidence of a higher moving rate, there also are some factors that tend to work against the trend. Corporations seem to be less likely to transfer employees from one market to another than they were ten years ago. And more employees are refusing intercity transfers because they are in two-career households. In these cases, what personnel directors call the trailing spouse cannot easily transfer his or her business or profession to a new city.

Families also are having fewer children, which may reduce their need for larger homes. All of these factors are discussed at length in other chapters. As with all trends, different influences are at play, and our job is to project which will have the strongest bearing on these specific trends throughout the next decade.

Taking all negatives and positives into account—and assuming we don't have a major recession—we still expect to see Americans moving at the rate of 20% a year in the 1990s. We will even go out on a limb and suggest that the age cohort with the lowest rate of moving, those 65 and over, will become more mobile in the years to come. The reason is that these senior citizens are in far better financial and physical shape than any other previous generation of retirees. They are more likely to have the resources and the stamina for a move. We expect that an increasing number of them will move away from their longtime homesteads to retirement homes, especially in temperate climates. The capital gains exclusion that the Internal Revenue Service allows for those over 55 who sell their homes is a contributing factor in the decision to move.

The high moving rate won't go on forever, though. When the Baby Boomers start hitting 65 in the second decade of the twenty-first century, the percentage of Americans moving will slow down considerably.

One important point to remember about people changing addresses is that very few of them move cross-country or even out of the region. International moves have increased in the past few years, but they aren't enough to make a major impact on the total rate. About two-thirds of the people who move stay in the same county, and 85% stay in the same state. The percentage who move from one major metropolitan area to another is less than 10% of the total.

Westward Ho, Southward Ho

It is no secret, of course, that the bulk of migration in this country has been to the West and the South. We will look at a few of the historical figures here simply because they are so basic to what has happened to our country since World War II. In light of our near-stagnant population growth, some of those statistics are also quite astounding.

In the 1950s the fastest-growing state in the United States was Florida, whose population increased by nearly 79%. In that one decade Florida moved from being the twentieth most populous state to the tenth. It advanced to ninth in 1970, seventh in 1980 and fourth by 1990. Here was a largely undeveloped swampland that rapidly turned into the postwar paradise for thousands of retired Americans. Retirees were attracted by the warm winters, low housing costs and very favorable state tax policies. They also knew about Florida because they had vacationed there, and obviously they liked it. Since then Florida's tourism business has grown tremendously, and the state has also attracted more than its share of businesses. All of this has created jobs, which attracts even more people, and the cycle of growth continues.

In the 40 years since 1950, our fastest-growing state on a percentage basis has been Nevada, up more than 570% in population. This obviously came on a very small base, as Nevada is still only the forty-third largest state in the Union. With a population of slightly more than one million, the whole state has about the same number of people as the New Orleans metropolitan area.

The other major percentage gainer over the past 40 years has been Alaska, which might surprise some readers—it is not exactly a sun-drenched playground. But the oil and gas finds of the 1960s and the building of the Trans–Alaska Pipeline in the 1970s attracted many fortune-seekers to the state. Alaska's population grew by about 350% between 1950 and 1990. Once again, Alaska is working on a small base with only about half the population of Nevada. It has, however, edged up from fiftieth to forty-ninth place in the past few years, leaving lonely Wyoming as the nation's least populous state.

In terms of sheer numbers, California boasts the greatest population increase of the past 40 years. It grew from about 10.5 million in 1950 to an estimated 29 million in 1990. Texas is another major gainer, moving from 7.7 million in 1950 to 17.7 million in 1990. Florida, meanwhile, grew from 2.7 million to 12.8 million.

In that 40-year span, only one of the 50 states actually has seen its population decrease. West Virginia had slightly more than two million residents in 1950, compared with 1.9 million in 1990.

Other states, while increasing in population, have obviously lagged the growth rate in the burgeoning states. For most of them, the growth has come internally rather than through migration from other states. There also are a few states, such as Iowa and the Dakotas, that have shown virtually no population increase over the past four decades.

Official Census Bureau projections indicate that the migration patterns and growth levels of the states will continue on the same trend into the twenty-first century. Unless someone makes a significant gold strike in North Dakota or Disney builds a major theme park in Iowa, those states have little chance of seeing their populations increase. Iowa, in fact, is projected to lose an average of more than 20,000 residents a year between 1990 and 2000. The 8% decline is expected to be the largest among the states. Pennsylvania is expected to have the largest numerical decline, averaging 35,000 persons a year during the decade.

State officials in Iowa dispute the Census Bureau projections and maintain that the state's population will stabilize in the coming decade. (Because no state wants to be noted for a population loss, disagreement with census figures is common.) If one were to add up the individual projections of the states, the U.S. population will be five million larger in 2000 than the U.S. Census Bureau projects. We will have to wait ten years to see which projections are closer to reality. Population projections for all 50 states plus Washington, D.C. are provided in the table on pages 114 and 115.

Sunbelt Slowing But Still Growing

Even though the rate of growth will subside considerably in the Sunbelt states, they will be the only states to have any substantial growth in the coming decade. The population increase in California, Texas and Florida will represent more than half of the country's total population growth between now and 2000.

The biggest percentage gain among the states in the 1990s will come in Arizona, whose population will expand about 23% to about 4.6 million in 2000.

California, already our most populous state, will maintain its ranking in 2000 and for the projectable future. There is no way California could lose this position unless, of course, three or four states merged into one. California will be the only top state to maintain its position in the next decade. Texas and Florida, moving up rapidly, are projected to pass up New York's stagnant population to become the second and third most populous states in the nation.

This population trend is going to cause some significant changes in our country in the twenty-first century. Perhaps the most important changes will be in the political arena, where the growing states will acquire more seats in the House of Representatives. When the 1990 Census Bureau figures come in, it is expected that New York and Pennsylvania each will lose three seats in the House, while Illinois, Michigan and Ohio will lose two each. California, meanwhile, will probably gain five seats, Texas will add four, Florida will add three, and Georgia and Arizona will pick up two each.

The pattern you see here isn't difficult to recognize. The old industrial states of the North are losing political clout to the emerging states of the South and West. Every time seats are shifted from one state to the next, the move is welcomed by the Republican party. That's because voters in recent years have overwhelmingly returned incumbents to office. With seats going to new states the Republicans will have an opportunity to run elections without facing entrenched Democratic incumbents. By 2000, which is five Congressional elections from now, the Republicans will have an excellent opportunity to chip away at the Democratic majority. If they defy all odds and overtake the Democrats, it will mark the first time since the 1953–54 session that the Republicans become the majority party in the House.

Another factor that should be considered is the mushrooming of the over-35 age group throughout the 1990s. If we can assume that older voters tend to vote Republican, the GOP might be able to boast a Republican president *and* Republican House of Representatives for the first time in 40 years. This obviously would have a seismic impact on American politics. Should it cause dyed-in-the-wool Democrats to worry about the future? Probably not. One thing that pundits have observed over the past 25 years is that the two political parties have edged closer together in their beliefs. Republicans generally are more liberal than they were 25 years ago, and Democrats more conservative. We are dealing with generalities rather than specifics here, so these statements are made with the full realization that there are many exceptions to the rule.

The other point that Democrats and Republicans both should remember is that voters also change party affiliations, something that has occurred with increasing regularity in the last few elections. One reason for this is the so-called one-issue candidate who might be a

Resident Population, 1950–1980, and Projected Population, 1990–2010 (in thousands)

Region, Division, and State or Other Area	1950	1960	1970	1980	1990	1995	2000	2010
U.S.	151,326	179,323	203,302	226,546	249,891	259,619	267,747	282,055
Region:								
Northeast	39,478	44,678	49,061	49,135	50,577	51,293	51,810	52,496
Midwest	44,461	51,619	56,589	58,866	59,777	59,867	59,596	59,018
South	47,197	54,973	62,812	75,372	87,276	92,366	96,919	104,919
West	20,190	28,053	34,838	43,172	52,261	56,093	59,422	65,622
N.E.	**9,314**	**10,509**	**11,848**	**12,348**	**13,078**	**13,466**	**13,775**	**14,243**
ME	914	969	994	1,125	1,212	1,247	1,271	1,308
NH	533	607	738	921	1,142	1,251	1,333	1,455
VT	378	390	445	511	562	579	591	608
MA	4,691	5,149	5,689	5,737	5,880	5,985	6,087	6,255
RI	792	859	950	947	1,002	1,029	1,049	1,085
CT	2,007	2,535	3,032	3,108	3,279	3,376	3,445	3,532
M.A.	**30,164**	**34,168**	**37,213**	**36,787**	**37,499**	**37,827**	**38,035**	**38,253**
NY	14,830	16,782	18,241	17,558	17,773	17,886	17,986	18,139
NJ	4,835	6,067	7,171	7,365	7,899	8,252	8,546	8,980
PA	10,498	11,319	11,801	11,864	11,827	11,689	11,503	11,134
E.N.C.	**30,399**	**36,225**	**40,262**	**41,682**	**42,055**	**42,041**	**41,746**	**41,111**
OH	7,947	9,706	10,657	10,798	10,791	10,742	10,629	10,397
IN	3,934	4,662	5,195	5,490	5,550	5,545	5,502	5,409
IL	8,712	10,081	11,110	11,427	11,612	11,625	11,580	11,495
MI	6,372	7,823	8,882	9,262	9,293	9,318	9,250	9,097
WI	3,435	3,952	4,418	4,706	4,808	4,811	4,784	4,713
W.N.C.	**14,061**	**15,394**	**16,327**	**17,183**	**17,722**	**17,825**	**17,850**	**17,907**
MN	2,982	3,414	3,806	4,076	4,324	4,426	4,490	4,578
IA	2,621	2,758	2,825	2,914	2,758	2,652	2,549	2,382
MO	3,955	4,320	4,678	4,917	5,192	5,304	5,383	5,521
ND	620	632	618	653	660	643	629	611
SD	653	681	666	691	708	711	714	722
NE	1,326	1,411	1,485	1,570	1,588	1,574	1,556	1,529
KS	1,905	2,179	2,249	2,364	2,492	2,515	2,529	2,564

Region, Division, and State or Other Area	1950	1960	1970	1980	1990	1995	2000	2010
S.A.	21,182	25,972	30,678	36,959	43,742	47,058	50,002	55,110
DE	318	446	548	594	666	702	734	790
MD	2,343	3,101	3,924	4,217	4,729	5,025	5,274	5,688
DC	802	764	757	638	614	620	634	672
VA	3,319	3,967	4,651	5,347	6,157	6,551	6,877	7,410
WV	2,006	1,860	1,744	1,950	1,856	1,786	1,722	1,617
NC	4,062	4,556	5,084	5,882	6,690	7,106	7,483	8,154
SC	2,117	2,383	2,591	3,122	3,549	3,740	3,906	4,205
GA	3,445	3,943	4,588	5,463	6,663	7,338	7,957	9,045
FL	2,771	4,952	6,791	9,746	12,818	14,189	15,415	17,530
E.S.C.	11,477	12,050	12,808	14,666	15,597	15,979	16,285	16,847
KY	2,945	3,038	3,221	3,661	3,745	3,745	3,733	3,710
TN	3,292	3,567	3,926	4,591	4,972	5,135	5,266	5,500
AL	3,062	3,267	3,444	3,894	4,181	4,307	4,410	4,609
MS	2,179	2,178	2,217	2,521	2,699	2,792	2,877	3,028
W.S.C.	14,538	16,951	19,326	23,747	27,937	29,329	30,632	32,961
AR	1,910	1,786	1,923	2,286	2,427	2,482	2,529	2,624
LA	2,684	3,257	3,645	4,206	4,513	4,517	4,516	4,545
OK	2,233	2,328	2,559	3,025	3,285	3,318	3,376	3,511
TX	7,711	9,580	11,199	14,229	17,712	19,012	20,211	22,281
Mt.	5,075	6,855	8,289	11,373	13,995	15,082	16,022	17,679
MT	591	675	694	787	805	798	794	794
ID	589	667	713	944	1,017	1,034	1,047	1,079
WY	291	330	332	470	502	495	489	487
CO	1,325	1,754	2,210	2,890	3,434	3,637	3,813	4,098
NM	681	951	1,017	1,303	1,632	1,809	1,968	2,248
AZ	750	1,302	1,775	2,718	3,752	4,218	4,618	5,319
UT	689	891	1,059	1,461	1,776	1,893	1,991	2,171
NV	160	285	489	800	1,076	1,198	1,303	1,484
Pac.	15,115	21,198	26,549	31,800	38,265	41,011	43,400	47,943
WA	2,379	2,853	3,413	4,132	4,657	4,841	4,991	5,282
OR	1,521	1,769	2,092	2,633	2,766	2,828	2,877	2,991
CA	10,586	15,717	19,971	23,668	29,126	31,463	33,500	37,347
AK	129	226	303	402	576	636	687	765
HI	500	633	770	965	1,141	1,243	1,345	1,559
PR	2,211	2,350	2,712	3,197				

Source: U.S. Bureau of the Census.

The Top 50 Metropolitan Statistical Areas and Primary Metropolitan Statistical Areas Ranked by Population Gain, 1987–2005 (in thousands)*

	Population		Change	Percent Change
	1987	2005	1987–2005	1987–2005
Los Angeles–Long Beach, CA	8,225.1	10,230.3	2,005.3	24.4%
Anaheim–Santa Ana, CA	2,255.5	4,141.0	1,885.5	83.6
Dallas, TX	2,397.7	3,827.2	1,429.4	59.6
Atlanta, GA	2,556.0	3,848.6	1,292.6	50.6
Oakland, CA	1,994.3	3,101.1	1,106.8	55.5
Tampa–St. Petersburg–Clearwater, FL	1,960.4	3,036.4	1,076.0	54.9
Phoenix, AZ	1,864.5	2,839.2	974.6	52.3
San Jose, CA	1,454.4	2,351.4	897.0	61.7
Denver, CO	1,693.9	2,529.5	835.5	49.3
Sacramento, CA	1,317.5	2,149.9	832.4	63.2
Washington, DC–MD–VA	3,541.0	4,367.6	826.6	23.3
San Diego, CA	2,196.5	3,011.9	815.4	37.1
Orlando, FL	919.1	1,712.4	793.3	86.3
Fort Lauderdale–Hollywood–Pompano Beach, FL	1,185.3	1,948.7	763.4	64.4
Nassau–Suffolk, NY	2,703.6	3,416.1	712.6	26.4
San Francisco, CA	1,587.4	2,254.1	666.7	42.0
Houston, TX	3,316.7	3,974.8	658.2	19.8
Minneapolis–St. Paul, MN–WI	2,307.7	2,922.1	614.4	26.6
West Palm Beach–Boca Raton–Delray Beach, FL	786.7	1,377.2	590.4	75.0
Riverside–San Bernardino, CA	2,017.6	2,592.2	574.5	28.5
Baltimore, MD	2,294.1	2,850.6	556.5	24.3
Miami–Hialeah, FL	1,784.8	2,320.3	535.5	30.0
San Antonio, TX	1,277.7	1,789.5	511.8	40.1
Seattle, WA	1,769.6	2,185.3	415.7	23.5
Middlesex–Somerset–Hunterdon, NJ	948.7	1,355.3	406.5	42.9
Austin, TX	688.7	1,085.7	397.0	57.6
Charlotte–Gastonia–Rock Hill, NC–SC	1,085.6	1,469.8	384.3	35.4
Raleigh–Durham, NC	651.4	1,034.4	383.0	58.8
Boston–Lawrence–Salem–Lowell–Brockton, MA	3,745.8	4,123.5	377.7	10.1
St. Louis, MO–IL	2,440.6	2,818.2	377.6	15.5
Fort Worth–Arlington, TX	1,227.1	1,581.7	354.6	28.9
Oklahoma City, OK	969.2	1,319.6	350.4	36.2
Norfolk–Virginia Beach–Newport News, VA	1,325.7	1,669.2	343.5	25.9

| | Population | | Change | Percent Change |
	1987	2005	1987–2005	1987–2005
Tucson, AZ	631.3	961.8	330.4	52.3
Atlantic City, NJ	312.1	634.6	322.5	103.3
Oxnard–Ventura, CA	639.6	933.4	293.8	45.9
Philadelphia, PA–NJ	4,831.5	5,124.9	293.4	6.1
Santa Rosa–Petaluma, CA	358.0	649.3	291.4	81.4
Columbus, OH	1,312.5	1,602.8	290.4	22.1
Santa Barbara–Santa Maria–Lompoc, CA	348.6	633.0	284.4	81.6
Salt Lake City–Ogden, UT	1,078.8	1,358.7	279.8	25.9
Greensboro–Winston-Salem–High Point, NC	919.8	1,197.0	277.2	30.1
Newark, NJ	1,859.8	2,127.5	267.6	14.4
Hartford–New Britain–Middletown–Bristol, CT	1,097.8	1,337.9	240.1	21.9
Monmouth–Ocean, NJ	940.6	1,177.1	236.5	25.1
Nashville, TN	929.0	1,154.2	225.1	24.2
Chicago, IL	6,160.0	6,378.4	218.4	3.5
Rochester, NY	1,011.0	1,217.6	206.6	20.4
Jacksonville, FL	846.9	1,052.8	205.9	24.3
Kansas City, MO–KS	1,509.5	1,715.2	205.7	13.6

*A metropolitan statistical area is a freestanding metropolitan area, while a primary metropolitan statistical area is a metropolitan area that is adjacent to at least one other.

Source: Woods & Poole Economics, Inc., Washington, D.C.

strong proponent of the environment or an opponent of legalized abortion. Strong stands like these can often attract voters from another party who agree with the candidate's position.

Voters will be far more independent and far less predictable in the coming decade. They will be far less likely to vote a straight party ballot than they were 20 years ago. The reason is that voters are more informed today than they were previously. They don't feel much loyalty to political parties and are far more interested in issues. Someone who didn't care much about Social Security when he was 35 might be a bit more concerned about it when he is 60. People don't think about child-care benefits until they have children, and others are opposed to Equal Employment Opportunities until they have been fired from their job because of age. These are the kinds of personal issues that make voters switch their allegiances.

One example of the impact that regions have on politics may be seen in those who have been elected to the presidency in the last 30 years. The last president not to come from a Sunbelt state was John F. Kennedy. Lyndon Johnson and George Bush came from Texas, Ronald Reagan and Richard Nixon from California and Jimmy Carter from Georgia. While Gerald Ford came from Michigan, he assumed the presidency after Richard Nixon resigned from office and lost in his election attempt.

Moving Toward a Bicoastal America

There is no question that the gradual shift of our population westward is going to erode the position of New York as the commercial, cultural and communications capital of the United States. Indeed, this has started to happen already, even though many New Yorkers still act as if they live in the center of the universe. In the past 30 years, scores of major corporations have moved out of the city. Many relocated to adjacent states such as Connecticut and New Jersey. But some major corporations, such as American Airlines and J.C. Penney, moved their headquarters to Texas. The corporate drain on New York City has been dramatic. It was home to 125 Fortune 500 companies in 1960, exactly one-fourth of the corporations on the list. But by 1989 the number had slipped to 48, representing less than 10% of the total.

Business figures also show that California has more rapidly growing corporations than any other state in the Union and is creating jobs at a faster rate. This is largely because California has attracted a large share of high-tech, aerospace, tourism and defense-related industries, all of which are growing at a steady clip. In its 1988 listing of the 500 fastest-growing companies in the country, *Inc.* magazine pointed out that 65 of the companies were in California, more than twice as many as any other state. Texas was second with 28 companies, and Florida was third with 27. These three states accounted for nearly one-fourth of the nation's emerging corporations.

It isn't sheer coincidence that these are also the fastest-growing states in terms of population. People generally follow jobs. It should also be noted that there is also an exception here. Pennsylvania, a state losing population, tied Florida with 27 companies on the fastest-growing list. There's no apparent explanation for this.

Although New York has a widely diversified economy, much of it is based on businesses that are not growing rapidly or are even shrinking. It has 19 companies on the list, fewer than the much smaller states of Georgia and Virginia. This doesn't mean that New York is going to dry up and blow away, but its influence on the rest of the country is definitely on the wane. By 2000 we will have become much more bicoastal and less dominated by the East Coast. The New York area will still be the most populous metropolitan area, but Los Angeles will be closing in on the Big Apple.

In 1970 the New York area, which includes parts of New Jersey and Connecticut, had more than 18 million residents, compared with 9.9 million in the Los Angeles–Orange County area. By 1985, New York had slipped to 17.9 million while Los Angeles was at 12.8 million. By a different measure Los Angeles County, with 8.3 million residents, already is larger than the five boroughs of New York, with 7.3 million. Los Angeles is growing faster, has more rapidly growing companies and is creating jobs at a higher rate.

One factor attracting business and people to the West Coast is the increased trade throughout the Pacific Rim. Major Japanese marketers such as Nissan and Toyota, for example, have established their U.S. headquarters in California. This escalation of trade with Asia and Australia will also have a positive effect on other West Coast metropolitan areas such as San Diego, San Francisco, Seattle–Tacoma and Portland, as well as Vancouver, British Columbia. For example, it was estimated in the mid-1980s that the unloading of foreign cars in Portland, Oregon created 1,800 jobs and pumped $82 million into the economy. One full-time job is created for every 223 cars that pass through the Portland docks.

If it weren't for its proximity to Washington, D.C. – a brief shuttle flight away – New York by now probably would have lost its position as the communications center of the country. While the ABC, CBS and NBC television networks are still based in New York, it's interesting to note that the newer networks, such as Cable News Network and Fox Broadcasting Co., are based, respectively, in Atlanta and Los Angeles.

A Crash with No Impact

The declining influence of New York on the rest of the country was demonstrated on October 19, 1987, the day the Dow Jones Industrial Average dived by more than 500 points. Most economists and analysts predicted that the crash would cause a recession and have a chilling impact on American industry. A year later it became evident that the crash had little if any impact outside New York's sphere of influence. Some layoffs occurred in the financial industry; some business strategies were altered because the market turned sour so quickly; and some financial advertisers disappeared from the *Wall Street Journal.* Nevertheless, the effect on Wall Street didn't extend to Main Street, USA.

There was a marked difference in impact felt from the 1987 crash and that from the 1929 crash. The latter helped thrust us into the Great Depression, which plagued this country for the next decade. The former reminded the rest of the country that what goes on in New York doesn't necessarily affect them.

Another aspect to this same phenomenon is the gradual regionalization of America. This is most evident among national consumer products companies that are putting increased influence and decision making on the regional level. One reason for this is the disparity in sales between different regions of the country. A brand of coffee that is the best-seller in one region might be in fourth place—or not even on the market—in another region. Even fast-food restaurant chains, which pioneered the nationalization of American eating, have started introducing regional uniqueness to their menus. This has been accompanied by more advertising dollars directed to local dealer groups and less to network television. Arby's, an Atlanta-based fast-food chain, completely dropped its national advertising in 1987 and pumped all of its promotional budget into regional advertising.

Throughout the next decade, regionalization will be the key strategy of many corporations that previously thought they could sell effectively on a national level. These companies will realize that there are countless regional differences that must be considered in the marketing process. Regional differences go beyond different tastes and customs. Some are more profound, such as the fact that average household income in the Northeast is $10,000 to $14,000 higher than in some states in the South and the Midwest. These are significant differences that marketers will have to address.

Where Will the Jobs Be?

There is no definitive answer as to where the most jobs will be in the coming decade. Most experts feel that high-tech and service businesses will create the bulk of new jobs in coming years. More recently, the decline in the dollar's value has made American products more competitive on world markets. This indicates that areas with export-related manufacturing will also do well, but manufacturing is expected to create no more than 5% of the new jobs in the 1990s.

Manufacturing jobs, once concentrated in a handful of midwestern and northeastern cities, will be spread more evenly around the country. Look for metropolitan areas below the top 20 to have the strongest job markets. Among them will be Tampa and Orlando, Florida; Phoenix, Arizona; Norfolk, Virginia; Salt Lake City, Utah; Oklahoma City, Oklahoma; and Austin, Texas. A report from the Conference Board listed several "big little cities," including some of those mentioned, that are positioned for faster growth in the coming years. Others include Cincinnati and Columbus, Ohio; Sacramento, California; Providence, Rhode Island; Fort Myers, Florida; Las Vegas, Nevada; and Charlotte, North Carolina.

Even the hard-hit Midwest is expected to regain some of its manufacturing punch if the lower dollar continues to make its products competitive on the world markets. All of these factors are a manifestation of regionalization in operation. And it is another blow to the centralized power and influence that New York has had on the rest of the country during most of the twentieth century.

Because of its sheer size, California will create the most jobs in the next decade. Texas also has potential to be a major job generator. Although its economy has become diversified in the last couple of decades, the state still depends heavily on petroleum, an industry whose future is tough to predict.

Florida also will create many jobs, but many will be in tourism, retail and services. Income levels for these are expected to be lower than in other states that will generate more technical, professional and skilled manufacturing jobs.

121

In discussing the economic health of various regions it is important to recognize that regions don't continually move upward or downward; they go along in cycles. Midwest manufacturing centers such as Chicago and Detroit thrived during the 1950s through the mid-1970s before being slammed by foreign competition. By the mid-1980s, these regions were starting to come out of their slumps.

Massachusetts started slipping a decade earlier than Chicago and Detroit, and by the mid-1970s started riding a crest of success due mainly to high-tech manufacturing. By the late 1980s, though, the state was facing economic problems again. Texas, Oklahoma and Louisiana have seen boom or bust several times during the twentieth century, but circumstance has always depended on the health of the petroleum industry. And the health of the petroleum industry has always depended on OPEC nations.

One factor that may have some impact on regional growth rates in the coming decade is the disparity in real estate values from one section of the country to another. Differences in home prices are common, of course—New York residences, for example, have always commanded higher prices than those in Peoria. But an unusual imbalance has come into play in the past few years. Housing prices on the West Coast have soared to the same heights as those in New York. Both coasts have seen steeper price rises than in the country's midsection. In 1988, for example, the median price of a home in Chicago was about $100,000, and other midwestern and southern cities were considerably below that. At the same time, median home prices in Los Angeles, San Francisco, New York, Boston and Washington were running closer to $200,000. This was the biggest disparity in prices ever registered between different sections of the country.

It is the demand for housing that causes prices to rise. However, it is reasonable to assume that prices will escalate to such a level that it will be difficult for people to afford living in certain areas. That is one of the reasons why New York's growth has peaked and companies have moved away, even if only to a neighboring state. If California housing prices continue to rise at the same steep rate, we can expect that companies there will start looking for alternative locations in the coming decade. The beneficiaries of pricey California real estate most likely will be Seattle, Portland, Phoenix and Salt Lake City.

From 'Burbs to Exurbs

Escalating home prices, coupled with an aversion to congestion, are going to result in a different kind of relocation in the 1990s. We expect that many companies, especially service-related industries, will move from inner cities or suburbs to exurbs. A Conference Board study indicated that "the borders of major urban business centers continue to move outward." Companies will plant themselves in smaller towns that are 50 to 150 miles away from major downtown areas. The reasons for this are lower living and operating costs and the fact that the companies need not be located downtown anymore. Technological advances such as computer networking, teleconferencing and facsimile transmission will allow the companies to communicate with central offices or with customers all over the world. This might well extend the exodus to the suburbs that has affected many major cities. Fifty years ago, corporate headquarters were generally located in downtown areas of major cities. First the executives started moving their families to the suburbs; then the middle managers followed suit. Eventually the corporate headquarters were moved to towns like Oak Brook, Illinois; Waltham, Massachusetts; and White Plains, New York.

In many major cities the migration of businesses to the suburbs has created a generation of reverse commuters. Many of them are young professionals living in trendy, regentrified city neighborhoods who commute to their jobs in the suburbs. As the young professionals get married they tend to move to suburbs closer to their jobs. Even more common than reverse commuters are those who commute from one suburb to another. One estimate has placed the number of suburb-to-suburb commuters at 25 million, nearly twice as many who commute from suburbs to a central city.

If the theory of the exurban exodus proves out, the employees can continue living in their suburbs and commuting to the semirural areas in which their companies have moved. A somewhat similar scenario is put forth by Jack Lessinger, an expert on real estate and urban development at the University of Washington at Seattle. He maintains that we will see a flight from the suburbs by a new kind of real estate consumer. "These consumers prefer the simple yet cosmopolitan lifestyle found in many non-metropolitan areas." He calls these areas "penturbia," because the exodus marks the fifth mass movement of Americans since the beginning of our nation. Says Lessinger: "Look for penturbia beyond the normal commuting range of the nation's central cities. It is small cities and towns, new subdivisions, homesteads, industrial and commercial districts interspersed with farms, forests, rivers and lakes."

We can accept Professor Lessinger's prediction of movement into the exurbs and some small towns. But using his own formula for the future, he also projects above-average growth in many rural areas of the country. This defies the 100-year-old trend of declining population and jobs in rural areas.

Despite huge gains in farm production, farm employment in the late 1980s numbered fewer than three million workers, compared with seven million in 1960. In 1920, 30% of our population lived on farms. By 1950 this had declined to 15%, and by 1990 it will be about 2%. If there is a return to the rural life in this country, we will have to see some kind of turnaround in this trend before we can predict that it will happen. So far, there has been no hint of a turnaround.

Americans still concentrate in relatively few population centers across the country. There are 37 metropolitan areas with populations of at least one million. These centers are home to nearly half of all Americans. For our own psychic welfare, the best place to live might well be in a small city. A study conducted in 1988 by Zero Population Growth, a Washington research organization, found that the bigger the city the higher the stress level of its inhabitants. Of 192 cities surveyed, the 22 with the highest quality of life all have populations of fewer than 200,000. Cedar Rapids, Iowa was tops on the list. The study assigned numerical values to social, economic and environmental factors of each city. Only one question remains unanswered: If these are such swell places to live, why don't more people live there?

Trends

- About one-fifth of all Americans move each year, and there's no sign of a slowdown until the Boomers start retiring in 20 years.

- The exodus to the Sunbelt will continue, with Florida, California and Texas accounting for more than half of U.S. growth in the 1990s.

- Population shifts will give more political clout to the Sunbelt.

- New York will slip in importance in the next ten years while Los Angeles will grow, giving us a bicoastal influence.

- Much of the next decade's most rapid growth will come in second-tier cities that are creating jobs rapidly. There also will be substantial growth in exurban areas and rural areas near big cities.

Strategies

- The tendency for American mobility will enhance all businesses related to moving, relocation, real estate, financing and transportation.

- Disparity in living costs should prompt employers to choose company locations carefully because home prices in some regions can be two or three times as high as in others.

- Because of regional variations, marketers will have to establish regional campaigns to sell products and services.

- With new communications technology, managers should consider moving to exurban areas to take advantage of lower cost and slower pace.

CHAPTER 9

Looking for Work in the Twenty-First Century

In 1989, *Changing Times* magazine carried a series of articles dealing with the economic progress of Americans. One of the articles was titled "Are We Becoming a Nation of Burger Flippers?" This wasn't intended as a flippant (excuse the play on words) headline. The question actually addressed a situation that had developed into a major controversy in the 1980s. The underlying question was, Could the service industry provide the same quantity and quality of jobs to make up for the shrinking number of manufacturing jobs? As in any controversy, there are no clear answers. There also are other questions that elicit conflicting answers from different sources: Can the U.S. economy thrive without a strong manufacturing base? Is manufacturing on the way back? Is the major industrial corporation a dinosaur? We will discuss these questions—and their answers— because they will have a profound impact on our economic status, our careers, our incomes and our lifestyles over the next 20 years. What is becoming more evident is that we face the same kind of workplace revolution going into the twenty-first century as we faced 100 years ago moving into the twentieth century. But instead of the Industrial Revolution of the past century, the United States is rapidly being engulfed by the Service Revolution.

One unusual characteristic of socioeconomic revolutions like these is that society doesn't realize they are taking place until they are well under way. The acceleration of the service sector as a segment of our economy has been going on since at least the end of World War II. But at that time we also were generating new manufacturing jobs. Our industrial sector, which had been geared up for the production of war materiel, was switching back to peacetime manufacturing. We were creating both manufacturing and service jobs. No one seemed concerned over the service jobs, however, until the number of manufacturing jobs started to decline around 1980. That decline will continue through the next decade.

Back in 1970, according to Bureau of Labor Statistics data, there were 19.4 million manufacturing jobs in the country and 11.4 million service jobs. (To avoid confusion, we will use the BLS definition, which excludes transportation, utilities, government, retail/wholesale, and financial services jobs from the service total.) Ten years later the number of manufacturing jobs edged ahead to 20.3 million. But the number of service jobs jumped ahead by nearly 54% to a total of 17.5 million. By 2000, the number of manufacturing jobs is projected to decline to 18.2 million while service jobs will soar to 32.5 million. With manufacturing jobs dropping by 10% and service jobs increasing nearly 200% in only 30 years, there is little doubt we are witnessing the Service Revolution. What we should expect is that this revolution will change our economy and our lives as much as the Industrial Revolution changed the lives and economy of our ancestors.

When we say that manufacturing jobs have declined we are referring to direct goods–producing jobs. Manufacturing generates many spinoff jobs, ranging from transportation to insurance, that won't decline. We will continue to make and ship goods in the foreseeable future, but manufacturers will employ fewer people to do it. When all statistics are taken into account, total employment in the United States is projected to increase from 111.6 million workers in 1986 to 133 million in 2000. This increase of about 19% is only about half the rate of growth in the prior 14 years. This is another indication that our economy is gradually slowing down, keeping pace with our decelerating population growth.

A century ago many decried the onset of the Industrial Revolution because it lured millions of workers away from farms and into the big cities. Today many decry the Service Revolution, but for a different reason. Service jobs, they say, do not pay as much as the manufacturing jobs they replace. A displaced steelworker making $35,000 a year probably wouldn't be happy as a hotel bellhop making $20,000 a year.

Critics point to statistics indicating that, while service jobs were overtaking manufacturing jobs in the 1980s the average weekly pay of American workers, after inflation, has not increased. The lower-paying service jobs, therefore, helped stifle any progress toward real income growth by the American worker. This reasoning is true, but it doesn't tell the whole story. There is no question that a person with a high school education or less can definitely make more money tending a blast furnace than flipping burgers. But that does not typify the kind of trade-offs American workers have been making. A substantial majority of the new service jobs created have been filled by women, many of whom were not previously working full-time. Very few women have ever held high-paying manufacturing jobs, but the sheer numbers of lower-paid women entering the work force has been enough to dilute any increase in real income levels.

Another point to remember is that not all service jobs pay inferior compensation. Our economy has also created a growing number of jobs for lawyers, computer programmers, psychologists, teachers, public relations specialists and many others that pay better-than-average wages. Therein lies one of the major differences between the Industrial Revolution and the Service Revolution. The Industrial Revolution created the opportunity for many uneducated workers to make a decent income and subsequently to achieve the American dream. In the closing days of the Industrial Revolution some of these uneducated workers—partly by joining together into labor unions— were able to bring home bigger paychecks than college professors. Such opportunities are rapidly waning, for there is far less potential for the uneducated and the unskilled to earn above-average wages in an economy dominated by the Service Revolution. The better-paying jobs will go to those with college educations and the most advanced technical skills. It is this imbalance that causes the most trauma among the working class. We are not creating high-paying jobs that can be filled by someone who doesn't have a high school education. A high school diploma might be considered a basic necessity in some cultures, but about one-fourth of adults in the United States did not finish high school.

The most critical problem is with those who have worked under the old system for most of their lives. Generally speaking, you can't expect a 55-year-old unemployed auto assembler without a high school education to learn how to be a computer programmer or investment banker. For these people—in fact for anyone without a college education or technical skill—the next decade will not offer much hope of improvement. They will have to compete for a shrinking number of higher-paying manufacturing jobs or be forced to accept jobs that pay less money than they are accustomed to. The rest of us should also realize that many of these once-productive workers may become a drain on society, through no fault of their own.

The figures we have considered so far do not tell the full story about the growth of the service sector. Other segments of what the BLS calls "service-producing" industries will also see a significant increase in jobs. There were 11 million retail jobs and 3.6 million financial services jobs in 1970. Both of these will at least double by 2000. The number of federal, state and local government jobs will increase from 12.6 million to more than 18 million.

What Happened to Manufacturing?

Before we look at the kind of jobs that will see the greatest demand in the next decade, we should look back to see why we lost so many manufacturing jobs. Could we have done something about it? Probably not. There is only one reason for the job loss: the high cost of manufacturing in the United States. Industry came up with two solutions to this challenge. The most obvious solution was the exportation of manufacturing jobs to other locations, especially Third World countries. Over the past 20 years, an increasing number of American manufacturers moved some or all of their operations offshore because they could hire workers at far lower wages. As a result, American stores are filled with merchandise that carry the labels of American companies but were manufactured in Taiwan, South Korea, Mexico, Ireland and a host of other countries that have an abundance of cheap labor.

The second solution was more economically sound. American manufacturers in the 1980s started making huge investments in updated manufacturing processes and equipment. They installed automated assembly systems and moved into the use of robotics. They increased productivity, but they did it by lowering the number of workers needed to put out the same quantity of products. That kind of investment makes more sense because the manufacturers will reap the rewards of investment in research and development for many years. Those who closed plants in Cleveland and opened new ones in Sri Lanka will enjoy only temporary benefits. As the dollar declined in value in the late 1980s, it led directly to higher labor costs in virtually every other country.

Manufacturers who built a plant offshore to serve a foreign market or to be closer to the source of national resources or component parts, will not be affected that greatly. But those who moved offshore only for cheap labor and are shipping manufactured products back to the United States may find in the next decade that they didn't save as much as they anticipated.

In the long run, labor-intensive manufacturing will gradually migrate from most industrialized countries to locations with less expensive labor and other operating costs. The devaluation of the dollar in the late 1980s will slow down that process somewhat. It is an inevitable aspect of the free enterprise system, however, that businesses will always be trying to cut their costs.

Some critics also contend that many of these companies lost their technological advantage when they went overseas. One example is the television set industry, which was exported to Japan in the 1960s and 1970s. When the videocassette recorder was developed the market was dominated by Japanese companies because they had been closer to television technology than American companies. In addition, some American companies that hired foreign firms to make their products found that their foreign suppliers started making similar products under their own labels and sold them in competition with the American-labeled products. In effect, American companies created their own competition.

Whether through offshore manufacturing or improved R & D, the bottom line for American labor was a decline in the number of jobs. As far as the next decade is concerned, workers should be assured that it is far more difficult to export service jobs than manufacturing jobs. We also are confronting a labor shortage in the next few years. We predict that American employers will press for higher immigration quotas so that they will have a bigger labor pool from which to choose.

Unions Fading Away

One side effect of the manufacturing decline in the United States has been the erosion of labor union membership. The union movement started more than 100 years ago to press for more pay and better working conditions for manufacturing workers. In this regard the unions were successful—by the 1950s America had the best-paid labor force in the world. They also had gained a multitude of benefits, ranging from pension plans to guaranteed annual incomes. But union existence also forced manufacturers to seek out new factory sites where they could find less expensive nonunion workers. Besides this, the federal government entered into the labor-management arena, creating laws that covered minimum wages, pension benefits, equal employment opportunities and safety in the workplace. Union people had pushed for these laws; and when the laws were enacted, they made unions less necessary.

In 1955, 33% of all nonagricultural workers in the United States were union members. This declined to 17% in 1987 and will probably be 10% to 12% by 2000. There has also been a drop in actual union membership, from 21 million in 1980 to about 17 million in 1987. Much of this represents the shift from manufacturing jobs to service jobs. The shifting job categories and drop in union membership is a phenomenon occurring not only here but in other industrialized countries of the world, including Japan. Some also was caused by technological advances. One example is in the newspaper business, where the once-powerful International Typographical Union was a force to be reckoned with. Organized in 1850 the ITU was the oldest national trade union established in North America. But as the old linotype machines were replaced by computer-driven electronic typesetting, the ITU was forced to merge into another union.

Another blow was dealt to the unions by their own members. The 1970s brought a jump in the number of decertification elections, in which members in particular companies voted on whether they wanted to remain in the union. The unions have been losing most of these elections. In some cases unions harmed themselves. For example, they resisted, rather than welcomed, the entry of women, minorities and part-time workers into their ranks. These elements make up the vast majority of new workers in the nation's jobs. The unions have tried to swim against the current and sign up new members, but they have been unsuccessful in organizing the fast-growing white-collar, technical and health care categories of workers. The only significant union gains have been among state and local government employees.

Unions may be a perfect example of an institution that has failed to respond effectively to changes in the environment. Realistically, maybe there is no way they can respond. Traditional reasons for their existence have evaporated. In a word, they are becoming irrelevant. If they expect to be a national force in the twenty-first century, unions will have to adopt and create new reasons for being.

Job-Hunting in the 1990s

Although another chapter discusses ethnic and demographic changes in our population during the next decade, we should take a brief look here at who will make up the work force in 2000. Minorities are projected to account for about 58% of the growth in the labor force between 1986 and 2000. Blacks will increase their share of the work force from 11% to 12%; Hispanics will grow from 7% to 10%; and Asians from 3% to 4%. But the "minority" making the biggest gains will be women, who will account for more than 60% of all those entering the work force. By 2000, 47% of all workers will be women, up from only 39% in 1972.

With a decline in the number of young people entering the work force, job hunting will become a shopper's market in the 1990s. The low unemployment figures reached in the late 1980s reflected the postrecession recovery, one of the longest on record, as well as the shortage of young job seekers. This is expected to help at least one chronic problem, the high unemployment rate among young black men.

A shortage of job-seeking youth doesn't mean a relative jump in salaries for lower-paying jobs. However, the ratio of jobs to workers should make it easier for any job seeker to get on someone's payroll. Based on statistics from the Bureau of Labor Statistics, the following occupations will register the biggest percentage gains between 1986 and 2000:

Occupation	No. of New Jobs (1986–2000)	% Increase
Paralegal	64,000	104%
Medical Assistant	119,000	90
Physical Therapist	53,000	88
Physical Therapy Assistant	29,000	82
Data Processing Equipment Repairer	56,000	80
Home Health Aide	111,000	80
Podiatrist	10,000	77
Computer Systems Analyst	251,000	76
Medical Records Technician	30,000	75
Employment Interviewer	54,000	71
Computer Programmer	335,000	70
Radiology Technician	75,000	65
Dental Hygienist	54,000	63
Dental Assistant	88,000	57
Physician Assistant	15,000	57
Operations and Systems Researcher	21,000	54
Occupational Therapist	15,000	52
Peripheral Data Processing Equipment Operator	24,000	51
Data Entry Keyer	15,000	51
Optometrist	18,000	49

These occupations are projected as having the highest percentage growth in the next decade. The important point to note is that virtually all of them require a professional background or special skill training. Also interesting is the fact that, with a couple of exceptions, the computer and health care fields dominate the leading categories.

Now let's take a look at the occupations that are projected to grow the most in actual number of jobs created between 1986 and 2000, also based on BLS data:

Occupation	Job Growth (1986–2000)
Salesperson (retail)	1,201,000
Waiter and Waitress	752,000
Registered Nurse	612,000
Janitor, Housekeeping Maid	604,000
General Manager, Top Exec	582,000
Cashier	575,000
Truck Driver	525,000
General Office Clerk	462,000
Food Counter and Related Worker	449,000
Nursing Aide, Orderly	433,000
Secretary	424,000
Guard	383,000
Accountant, Auditor	376,000
Computer Programmer	335,000
Food Preparation Worker	324,000
Teacher (elementary)	299,000
Receptionist, Information Clerk	282,000
Computer Systems Analyst	251,000
Cook (restaurant)	240,000
Licensed Practical Nurse	238,000
Gardener, Groundskeeper	238,000
Maintenance Repairer	232,000
Stock Clerk	225,000
First-Line Supervisor, Manager	205,000
Dining Room, Cafeteria Attendant	197,000
Electrical and Electronic Engineer	192,000
Lawyer	191,000

As you can see, there are no manufacturing or related jobs among the fastest growing. Besides that, most of the jobs requiring little or no special skills are also low-paying. The only exception to that may be truck driver. The most critical occupational shortage in the next decade undoubtedly will be for registered nurses. By the late 1980s shortages had already developed in many areas of the country. Nationally, more than 10% of nursing jobs were vacant in 1989.

According to *Modern Healthcare,* the industry's leading journal, the situation has forced hospitals into full-blown marketing campaigns to attract nurses. Hospitals have engaged in every form of advertising, from direct mail to television. Some have run contests to entice applicants, and others have promised cash bonuses — in addition to 20% higher pay — for those who work the night shift for one year. Given this condition, can you imagine how difficult it will become in the next decade when another 612,000 jobs for registered nurses will be created by the health care industry? It will force the participants into dramatic measures to recruit men and women into nursing and keep them there.

Going Where the Jobs Are

This situation demonstrates what is growing into a major problem for the United States. Many young people are not being directed (by parents, teachers, counselors and such) into fields where there is the greatest need. There is good cause, of course, for them to shun fields like nursing and secretarial, where wages are traditionally low and there's little chance to step up to a higher job. It also doesn't help matters that nurses and secretaries are working next to doctors and executives who may be making ten times as much money as they are. Why are they paid so little? One reason, no doubt, is because those fields have been dominated by women. Not until substantial numbers of men enter those fields — or until the shortage hits the crisis stage — can you expect salary levels to increase.

The mismatch of education to jobs is taking place even in computer and engineering fields, where pay levels are higher and opportunity for advancement exists. Among college graduates with bachelors degrees, engineers already attract the highest starting salaries, but that apparently hasn't been enough to attract a sufficient number of newcomers.

Having listed the fastest-growing occupations we should also report on those projected to have the biggest declines by the end of the 1990s. According to the BLS, here are the major losers:

Occupation	No. of Jobs Lost (1986–2000)	% Decline
Electrical and Electronic Assembler	133,000	−54%
Electrical Semiconductor Processor	15,000	−51
Railroad Conductor, Yardmaster	12,000	−41
Railroad Brake, Signal, Switch Operator	17,000	−40
Gas, Petroleum Plant Worker	11,000	−34
Industrial Truck, Tractor Operator	143,000	−34
Shoe Sewing Machine Operator	11,000	−32
Telephone Station Installer, Repairer	18,000	−32
Chemical Equipment Controller	21,000	−30
Chemical Plant, System Operator	10,000	−30
Stenographer	50,000	−28
Farmer	332,000	−28
Statistical Clerk	19,000	−26
Textile Machine Operator	55,000	−25
Central Office, PBX Installer	17,000	−23
Farm Worker	190,000	−20
Coil Winder, Taper, Finisher	6,000	−19
Central Office Operator	8,000	−18
Directory Assistance Operator	5,000	−18
Compositor, Typesetter, Arranger	5,000	−17

One thing that has been constant over the past 100 years is the decline of jobs in farming. This isn't because we are eating less food but because agriculture is one of the most productive industries in this country. It has been transformed in the twentieth century from a largely labor-intensive business to one that is highly mechanized, automated, systematized and computerized. A sign of progress in any industry is the production of more goods with less labor.

Many of the other big losers, as expected, are in some segment of manufacturing. This is a good point at which to reiterate a question asked at the beginning of this chapter: Can the United States continue to thrive if its manufacturing base fades away? There are those, including many eminent economists, who say that the United

States cannot survive without manufacturing, that we cannot have a pure service economy where we go around shining each other's shoes and serving each other meals. We must make things and sell them to create wealth in this country. That notion is still true today but is becoming less true as we meander down the road to the twenty-first century. A hundred years ago there were those who said that agriculture was the linchpin of our economy. We would always need hordes of workers to pull the food from the earth and to tend the sheep and cattle. The role of agriculture obviously has changed. Now the role of manufacturing in our economy is changing.

What is interesting to note is that manufacturing's share of the gross national product has remained virtually unchanged—at 21% to 22%—for the past 35 years. During that same span manufacturing's share of the country's employment has declined from 34% to less than 20%. Manufacturing has continued to create wealth without creating new jobs.

We exist today in a world economy. An American company can manufacture here or in Mexico. Either way it produces wealth, although by manufacturing in Mexico, it also produces wealth for that country. A huge proportion of the goods sold in the United States are made abroad. In effect, that makes us the producer's salesperson. And sales is an honorable profession. What we are doing very gradually is learning how to thrive without traditional smokestack industries. We can become the world's salesperson, shipper, architect, financier, management consultant, marketer, communicator, teacher, technologist, doctor, lawyer and accountant; eventually we will be able to survive and to thrive without traditional industries.

We probably will have a major manufacturing component in our economy for decades to come, but it will evolve into a new form of manufacturing, very technologically oriented. In fact, the new technique will be a hybrid of manufacturing and technology. Run by scientists rather than shop foremen, its employees will be robots rather than humans. It will be knowledge-intensive and capital-intensive rather than labor-intensive. Rather than lathes, blast furnaces and extrusion machines, the tools of the new manufacturing will be lasers, microwaves, fiber optics, nuclear power, parallel processing, particle accelerators, artificial intelligence, superconductors and other technologies on the cutting edge of science and industry.

That leads directly to the next question: Will manufacturing ever return to the United States? If manufacturing is going to return to our economy, it will be in the high-tech mode described above. As a result, it will not create the millions of jobs that steel mills, auto plants, airplane factories and textile mills created earlier in this century. If the dollar continues to become devalued in the coming decade, we might be able to hold on to some manufacturing business for a while, but manufacturing inevitably is headed toward the Third World. And those who complain most about it – the manufacturers – are the ones making that inevitability come about. What is likely to happen in the twenty-first century is that manufacturers will continue to seek less expensive factory locations. Japan, Taiwan, South Korea, Hong Kong and Singapore will be priced out of the market. Manufacturers will search out undeveloped and primitive lands to build new plants. Cheap labor, however, will not be enough; they also must provide the upgraded technology, which will be a major U.S. export in the years to come.

Exports, of course, will become more important in the next decade because of the growing world economy. Agriculture will be a key player in the export picture because we have the resources to fill the world's demand for food. That will create wealth for the United States but will not create any additional farming jobs. We also will export technology, information, marketing skills, education and many other functions we have developed in the past 20 years.

An Unbalanced Equation

We can't discuss job opportunities of the 1990s without taking a look at the educational level of those who will be filling the jobs. The news on that front is mixed. On the positive side it should be noted that in 1985, the United States set a record when 75% of those 25 and over were estimated to be high school graduates. This was a remarkable turnaround from 1940, when only 25% of our adult population had high school diplomas. On the negative side we also must point out that a high school diploma won't be sufficient for most of the jobs being created in the next decade. Far more jobs will be in computer programming, law, health care, management and other fields where a college education is necessary. But only 20%

of Americans 25 and over have college degrees. Even when they go to college, Americans seem to be ignoring the fields that offer the best opportunities for the future. A major anomaly is occurring in science and engineering, where a projected increase in jobs is being met by a decline in college majors.

An American Council on Education study conducted in conjunction with the University of California at Los Angeles shows that the percentage of freshmen interested in science majors has dropped by one-third over the past 20 years. Mathematics, a foundation for many of the sciences and engineering, is attracting only .06% of the freshmen, a dive of 80% since 1966. Particularly hard hit are the fast-growing fields of computer programming or systems analysis. They peaked in 1981, when more than 8% of the freshmen expressed interest in them. By 1987, this had slipped to less than 3%. Even with more women going into engineering, that major has also declined in interest, attracting only 8.5% of the freshmen in 1987, compared with 12% in 1981.

What are the students interested in? The big winner is business, the major mentioned by nearly one-fourth of incoming freshmen. Also growing is the percentage of freshmen who say they want to go into teaching. Faced with this situation, employers who need technical workers will have to take drastic measures. They should start recruiting on the high school level, persuading students to go into the sciences and perhaps even offering them scholarships to do so. If the law of supply and demand prevails, we also can expect to see far higher entry-level salaries for those in technical areas.

Employers certainly will have to become more involved in the educational process to ensure a steady flow of new workers. One area that appears ready for a big boost is adult education, much of which will be subsidized by employers. Those in the 35-to-54 age group are the most likely to avail themselves of public education, and that will be the country's fastest-growing cohort in the 1990s. Employers will have to spend more on adult education and job training in the 1990s. They also will have to look at older Americans as a target for that training in the hopes that they will be able to replace some of the shortfall in entry-level workers.

The bottom line regarding education, regardless of major, is that the investment of time and money is worth it. That is true for individuals as well as for employers. The U.S. Census Bureau estimates that those with college degrees average nearly twice as much annual income as those with high school diplomas. The differential is even wider for those with professional degrees, who average almost three times as much as high school graduates. The use of the word *investment* was purposeful. The price of a college education has risen steeply in the past two decades. Tuition, room and board at top-ranked universities was running close to $20,000 a year in the late 1980s. This probably will jump to about $30,000 by the end of the century, but it will still be a good investment.

The Big Corporation as Dodo Bird

The last of the questions regarding American business deals with the fate of major industrial corporations. Much of American industry today is like an overweight and overaged heavyweight — big, slow to respond, inflexible, unable to maneuver gracefully. It's not what it used to be. As of the mid-1980s, small businesses had caught up with big businesses in terms of employment. For the first time in this century, more private sector workers were in businesses with fewer than 100 employees. Between 1980 and 1986, the number of employees working at companies with more than 1,000 employees had declined by 9%. At the same time, the work force at companies with fewer than 100 employees had gone up by 17%.

The trend toward more service businesses in the coming decade bodes well for small businesses. Service businesses generally do not need the huge capital investments that manufacturing businesses do. Service businesses also may provide specialized or personal services that a small operation can deliver more effectively than a large corporation.

Another aspect of small business that is growing dramatically is franchising. Although they may operate under the trademarks of well-known national companies, most franchise outlets are owned locally and are an important element in the growth of small business. Franchising might also prove to be the perfect business marriage, with one partner providing the expertise, marketing and national reputation, and the other partner providing local ownership and attention to detail. Look for franchising of many new kinds of businesses in the coming years.

The small-business sector is largely being fueled by a growth in entrepreneurial companies. Many of these are self-employed persons, a category that is growing far faster than salaried workers. Some of these, of course, are those upper and middle management people who were squeezed out of big corporations during the downsizing of the 1980s. This squeezing of corporate management levels most certainly will continue through the 1990s. For years, small businesses tried to imitate big businesses. Now, big businesses realize that they have become enmeshed in bureaucratic mazes that rival those of the federal government. What the big guys are trying to do in effect is to imitate the little guys and get rid of layers of management.

Major corporations may slim down in the next ten years, but they will not disappear in the twenty-first century. These behemoths of business, however, will become less important to our economy. The real action of the next decade will occur in the small-business sector.

ADVISORY

Trends

- The number of manufacturing jobs is declining, while service jobs are proliferating rapidly.

- Labor union membership and influence are eroding rapidly.

- The labor shortage of the 1990s will attract more women and minorities into business and will keep the unemployment rate low.

- American students are shunning science and technology, two areas of high job growth in the next decade.

- Most of new job generation is coming from small companies, while big companies are shrinking their work forces.

Strategies

- Manufacturing workers should prepare for possible dislocation. Retraining in service occupations will be the best alternative.

- Major growth in manufacturing jobs will be in robotics, automation, computers and other high-paying engineering specialities.

- College students should consider majoring in subjects with the greatest job potential, such as medical, computer and legal fields.

- Job seekers should enhance their educations with special training in computers and services.

- State and local governments should shift economic development emphasis to the formation of small companies rather than using incentives to entice big companies. Major corporate payrolls are shrinking.

PART 3

THE AMERICAN MARKET:
A MOVING TARGET

CHAPTER 10

The Challenge of Predicting American Taste

In speculating what our society will be like in 2000 A.D., some projections are relatively easy to make, and they are virtually certain to occur. For instance, if there has been a decline in the number of teenagers during the 1980s then there will be fewer people in their 20s during the 1990s. But other projections are more difficult to make—for example those dealing with the taste and lifestyle of the American public. H. L. Mencken said: "No one ever went broke underestimating the taste of the American people." But a lot of companies went broke trying to develop products that would suit the American taste. Consumer product companies have learned many times over that there is no foolproof way to predict how the public will react to a new item placed in the market. That is why as many as three-fourths of new consumer products are unsuccessful. Perhaps one of the most publicized lessons involved the Coca-Cola Co. a few years back. This was a company, remember, that rode the crest of popularity for 100 years while its flagship brand was the best-selling soft drink in the world. That is a remarkable achievement and a testament to Coca-Cola's marketing prowess.

During the 1980s, however, the company realized it was gradually losing market share to its primary rival, Pepsi-Cola. Coca-Cola conducted extensive research on consumer preferences and discovered that in blind taste tests most Americans liked a slightly different taste. This research led them to change the Coke formula for the first time in its century-old history. This wasn't done quietly but in the midst of a massive publicity campaign. What followed was a firestorm of criticism against Coca-Cola; it could be described as nothing less than a consumer uprising against a company that was the leader in its field. Americans wanted nothing to do with the "new Coke"; they wanted the old Coke. Coca-Cola dug its heels in and said no, the Coke formula was being changed no matter how many grass-roots pressure groups were springing up across the country. Within months Coca-Cola learned an old but valuable lesson: The customer is always right. The company stubbornly kept its new Coke on the market but also reintroduced its old formula labeled "Classic Coke." Even though the company spent far more money promoting the new Coke, more Americans continued to ask for and buy Classic Coke. This version alone became the best-selling soft drink in the country. Recent sales figures compiled by *Beverage Digest* show that the new Coke is wallowing in tenth place among all soft drinks. There was no way that Coca-Cola could know in advance that the formula change would provoke such a negative public reaction.

We point out this real-life example to demonstrate that many of the projections, predictions and guesses made in this chapter are subject to the whims of the American public. But we can't ignore those whims. This book is more interested in trends than fads, but we cannot ignore the fact that the United States has developed into a nation of fads, an important characteristic of this country. Certainly other countries have fads, but none comes close to the ongoing parade of gimmicks, sparks, rages, kicks, wrinkles and flashes that permeate our society. In most other countries, certainly in Europe and the Far East, there is a more abiding sense of tradition, where it seems a greater asthetic (although not necessarily monetary) value is placed on classical music, art and literature. Americans, on the other hand, are constantly on the prowl for new, avant-garde things. Note, however, that although other countries are more cautious about fads, they sometimes do take a plunge once in a while and even start some of them.

We treat fads differently. As a society we tend to embrace a fad in our aggregate arms, squeeze the hell out of it, then drop it and move on to the next fad. The major reason for this is that American marketers have an inexhaustible supply of new products that they

throw at us. We sometimes whip ourselves into a frantic state, trying to keep up with all the new and passing fashions, appliances,
status symbols, rock groups, television stars, hip sayings, haircut
styles and so forth.

One prediction is that the American penchant for fads will diminish in the 1990s. By the early part of the twenty-first century our
attitude toward fads will be very similar to the European view. That
will occur because we are becoming more like our European cousins,
and they are becoming more like us. Because Americans and Europeans travel more we will learn more about each other, which is how
cultures intermingle. European standards of living are growing faster
than ours, so they will catch up with us — and probably pass us — in
economic terms. But those are only secondary reasons. We will become less fad-driven because of our aging population. The fad craze
exploded in the 1960s and 1970s because we had so many young
Baby Boomers then, and the young are more receptive to fads than
the old. Going into the twenty-first century, there will be far fewer
young people and far more older people. Older people tend to hang
on to things that were important to them while they were young. That's
already happening. The "Big Chill" generation has created an industry devoted to worship of the 1950s and 1960s. Beatles records are
still played on rock music stations more than 25 years after they were
first heard in this country. Nostalgia will be a growing industry because there will be more middle-age people to be nostalgic. During
the youth boom of the 1950s and 1960s there was no great nostalgia
kick for the 1930s and 1940s. Radio, in fact, is a mirror of American
society. There is plenty of contemporary rock on the air, but an increasing number of stations are playing golden oldies and soft rock
for the 35- to 45-year-olds and even "music of your life" for those
55 and over. There is more talk radio and all-news radio, both of
which appeal to predominantly older audiences. These formats will
proliferate even more in the future, corresponding with the increase
in the number of older people.

Brand Loyalty Rebounds

For many years marketers have been concerned about a marked
decline in brand loyalty among American consumers. DDB Needham

Worldwide, a major advertising agency, has conducted a lifestyle study tracking consumers since 1975. In that first year 80% of married men and 74% of married women were classified as "brand loyal"; that is, they tried to stick to well-known brand products. By the early 1980s these figures had slipped to 62% for men and 56% for women. But by the late 1980s the numbers started edging upward again. We believe that brand loyalty will continue its upward swing because younger people are more open to change and experimentation. They are more likely to try new products whereas older consumers are more likely to find something they like and stick to it.

Backing up the DDB Needham study are the sales figures of generic products, which are the antithesis of brand-name goods. Their sales should run counter to the trend of brand loyalty; and they do. Sales of generic grocery products peaked at 2.4% of all dollar sales in 1982 and have since slipped to less than 1.1%. There has been a notion that older people tend to buy generic products because they are less expensive than brand-name items. That was true during the 1981–82 recession, but they are doing it to a lesser degree today. Why? Because older people are changing. Senior citizens of the 1970s don't have very much in common with senior citizens of the 1990s. Older people are better off economically today than they were ten years ago. Besides that, it was the rapid inflation of the late 1970s that prompted food retailers to stock generic products in the first place. Inflation has since subsided and is not expected to return at such high levels through the 1990s. Within a couple of years the generic products will disappear from most supermarkets except, perhaps, for some commodity items such as plastic trash bags, paper towels, paper plates, salt and such. Faring somewhat better than generics will be the retailers' private label merchandise. These will be more attractive to the older consumer because they promise a modicum of quality along with lower prices. Generics were sold strictly on their low cost merits.

Another reason for the growth of brand products in the years to come is the fact that more men are food shopping or doing it all themselves. Despite conventional wisdom the DDB Needham study shows that men are more brand conscious than women. Some researchers feel that the opposite is true, but evidence is weighing in against them. What appears to be occurring is a subtle shift in this brand consciousness of American shoppers. Instead of being loyal to a particular brand consumers have established their own array of "acceptable brands" in specific product categories. Every one of the brands will serve their needs—and they may even have a favorite— but they most often will buy the one that is on sale. Soft drinks and beer are both excellent examples. In any given week the biggest-selling beer or soft drink is the one on sale. But customers are less likely to drop down to a brand they haven't heard of, no matter how low the price.

A major strategy that brand products have used to combat generics, as well as other brand competitors, is money-saving coupons. Studies show that more than three-fourths of all households use coupons, and redemptions were increasing in the 1980s by about 10% a year. Marketers also have added rebates and cents-off packaging to coupons as a price incentive to shoppers. This combination of brand name quality and a "bargain" price is an effective marketing tool for the mature consumer. Besides the success of couponed products, the same combination has helped the upscale factory outlet stores develop into a hot marketing concept. Another similar retail trend developing in some parts of the country is the warehouse club. Food and dry goods are displayed in packing boxes; some are sold in bulk quantities; and prices are at discount levels. All will flourish because of the combination of brand names and lower prices. This technique shows no sign of letting up in the next decade.

Consumers have developed a great appetite for "deals." Many retailers, even upscale ones, have remarked that they have difficulty attracting shoppers into their stores unless they run deep-discounting sales. The best evidence of this trend perhaps can be found in recent moves by two of the nation's largest retailers—Sears, Roebuck and Montgomery Ward. In the past couple of years both companies have adopted a new policy of carrying brand-name products and selling them at discount prices. Sears trumpeted the change in March 1989 by dramatically closing all of its stores on one day and reopening them with the discounted brand-name policy. This was a revolutionary change of philosophy by Sears, which had prided itself for years in carrying only private label merchandise. That policy was successful for decades; and then, not so suddenly, Sears started losing its huge market share. What happened? The inevitable. American consumers

149

changed—slowly, perhaps imperceptibly, but they changed. Even with all of its resources Sears failed to realize this gradual transition with its shift in buying habits, patterns and motivations. In the years to come, Sears's 1989 shift in policy will be viewed as the strategy that saved the company. Without it Sears might not have been around to welcome the twenty-first century.

Returning to the supermarket business for a moment we should point out that researchers are also noticing a developing trend of store loyalty that didn't exist before. Today's shoppers—many of them in two-income households—simply don't have the time to cruise the sales at several supermarkets, so they select one as their basic provider and do virtually all their shopping there.

The Case for Quality

During the lengthy economic recovery after the 1982 recession marketers noticed that Americans were responding more positively to a higher level of quality in products. This covered virtually every consumer product from Porsche sports cars to Godiva chocolates. One demographic group in particular—the overpublicized Young Urban Professionals, better known as Yuppies—were stereotyped as being selfish because they lavished luxuries on themselves. If that contention were true it should have come as no surprise. These young people were knocking down record high salaries right out of college. They were getting married years later than those in the previous generation, and even after they got married they waited longer to have their first child. And increasingly, they had only one child or no children. Result: They became the luxury marketer's dream because they had a lot of discretionary income. They also were trendsetters, however, and what this demographic sliver identified as being fashionable rubbed off on similar demographic groups. Whether they were selfish is not important to this discussion. What is significant is that Yuppies contributed to a trend in which the value of a product's quality was more important than price or any other individual factor. In other words, they demanded the best.

The result of all this was the flourishing of a generation of products that even with their quality appeared overpriced to the average

American. The difference between the prices of these items and what they really were worth could denote their status or cachet. A certain mystique was attached to ownership of specific brands of products. For example the BMW, a fine automobile, almost became a joke in the 1980s because it was regarded as a "Yuppiemobile." It was the epitome of automotive excellence, and its sales soared; but its models also carried sticker prices two or three times those of Japanese cars of similar size and equipment. But the BMW was perceived as having more quality—and an added dash of prestige.

Another product of the 1980s was Perrier sparkling water. In some restaurants the price of a small bottle of Perrier was nearly as much as a cocktail or glass of wine. Club soda was less expensive than Perrier, had the same number of calories and arguably similar taste; yet millions of Americans continued asking for Perrier because it was perceived as having more quality and a glimmer of status.

The question that marketers ask is whether this thirst for over-priced, status-bearing products will continue to boom throughout the 1990s. The answer is easy: No. We feel confident about that because the number of people entering their Yuppie years, say 25 to 35, will be 10% less than it was a decade ago. This alone will diminish demand by 10%.

The lower value of the dollar will also contribute to the decline in sales of prestige items because the prices of many imported goods will move beyond the reach of many Americans. That was already witnessed in 1988 and 1989 with a decline in the sales of luxury imported cars. We also might see in the next few years the first serious marketing miscalculation by the Japanese car makers. Nissan and Toyota were both introducing new luxury models in late 1989, just as the American appetite for cars in the over-$30,000 category seemed to be sated. The best formula for any company that wants to be successful in the 1990s is to marry the perception of product quality image with a fair price. The factory outlet mentality being developed by American consumers will make it very difficult for faddish products to continue selling at unbelievably high prices. They won't disappear, of course. There will always be someone who pays top dollar for prestige goods, but there will be fewer of them in the 1990s than there were in the 1980s.

Service: The Ultimate Luxury

Of all the commodities in the world, the one that is becoming rarer and more expensive than any other is service. Year after year, one American industry after another has cut back on customer service. In some cases, service has been eliminated altogether. Before World War II, for example, there was little grocery "shopping" in this country. A customer went into the local grocery store and approached a clerk—often the store's owner or a family member—and asked for a specific product, sometimes by brand name. If the request was for Ivory Flakes, for instance, the clerk would pluck the product off of the shelf and put it on the counter. As the customer went down the list the clerk in turn would fetch the products and place them on the counter. When the list was fulfilled the clerk would add up the bill on a brown paper bag, put the groceries into the bag and collect the payment. At the time those neighborhood grocery stores were being threatened by a new concept that was going to drive them out of business: the supermarket. Younger readers should not confuse the supermarket of the 1930s with those that exist today. Yesterday's supermarkets were larger than the grocery stores, but only a fraction of the size of supermarkets today. They generally offered a greater variety of goods, but what made them novel was that consumers were able to walk through the two or three aisles and take the products off the shelves themselves. This retail technique accomplished two goals at one time. It provided a wider range of products and allowed consumers to compare competing brands. It also enabled the grocer to take care of more customers and sell more merchandise without hiring extra workers. That also allowed the supermarket manager to mark down prices a bit and entice even more customers into the store.

The supermarket marked a milestone in two major parallel trends that still are wielding their influence on society. We continue to have a greater variety of products from which to choose, and we are getting less personal service in virtually every area. The self-service supermarket came into its own in the postwar years. Following close behind was the self-service mass merchandiser store, or discount store. Customers pawed through racks of clothing, tried them on in fitting rooms, checked themselves out in the mirror and decided whether they liked the look. The first time the customer came in contact with a human being was at the checkout counter. Those too young to remember anything before the days of self-service retailing should consider the service station. It wasn't too long ago—less than 15 years—that we drove into a station and told the attendant to "fill 'er up." While gasoline was being pumped into the tank the attendant cleaned the car windows and checked the oil. He even checked tire pressure if asked. Today more than three-fourths of us serve as our own attendants—pumping our own gas, wiping our own windshields and checking our own oil. We might not like doing those chores, but many gas stations no longer have attendants. At others the cost of full service may be 50 cents a gallon higher than self-service (maybe they shouldn't call them "service" stations anymore).

Even more recently, millions of Americans have been introduced by their banks to automated teller machines (ATMs) or cash machines. You put in your cash card, punch in your personal code and then make a deposit or withdrawal, pay a bill, transfer funds or even take out a small loan. Every time a customer deals with an ATM signifies one less transaction he or she is making with face-to-face contact with a bank teller.

Of greater significance, American consumers are getting far less personal service in most of their business dealings. Because the supply of service is shrinking in so many areas it contributes to a greater value, both monetary and physical, being placed on personal service. A haircut, manicure or massage has a distinctly higher value today than it did 40 years ago in that we get a human being's undivided personal attention for an hour or half-hour.

This trend toward curtailed service will not only continue but will accelerate in the 1990s. Some of it will be caused by industry trends, such as the growth in vending machines. For decades vending machines have dispensed snacks, cigarettes, newspapers, soft drinks and coffee. In the future vending machines will be used for more expensive products. They already are a major means of dispensing rental videotapes. Improved technology will provide us with vending machines that will sell frozen food entrees at 24-hour vending centers. The machines will be able to accept larger demoninations of bills and make change. Pantyhose, film, magazines, pocketbooks and many other items also will be moving into vending machines in the next few years.

As we move into the 1990s the same kind of polarization that has occurred in regard to prices will also apply to service. An increasing number of businesses will eliminate personal service by turning functions over to machines and computers. At the other pole the demand for personal service will grow, sometimes because service is eliminated at the lower levels. It is difficult enough for the average man to shop for a personal gift for his spouse, spouse-equivalent or friend. It is even more difficult at a retail store with no personal service or with unprofessional minimum-wage clerks. That has led to the increase in executive shopping services that many upscale retailers offer to men. For some reason there aren't as many services offered to women who want to shop for men. We predict those will increase sharply in the next decade as more women rise into executive ranks.

As social animals most normal Americans crave personal contact; we can't live contentedly in a world of machines. The curtailment of personal service in so many areas probably will lead to a greater demand for other services that can be provided by personal consultants. These personal consultants would include fitness trainers, dieticians, cosmetologists, communications specialists, travel consultants and tutors.

We also predict the beginning of a new industry of household consultants or managers. These service people will perform a wide range of chores that previously were left to a nonworking spouse. These managers will collect bids from tradespeople, supervise home repair and maintenance, shop for gifts for special occasions and plan dinner parties. We already have spawned categories of household consultants, from financial planners to counselors who help high school students select a college.

The fact that the number and percentage of women in the work force will continue to grow in the 1990s will provide more impetus for this trend. The fact that there will be more two-income households in the future will make these services economically feasible for a greater number of families.

The Convenience Factor

The elimination of personal service from various areas of business doesn't necessarily mean that the consumer will get worse service.

In fact, it may mean just the opposite. Automated teller machines, for example, allow us to withdraw cash around the clock. Machines also have been installed in department stores, airports and major office buildings, making them very convenient for users. It is this convenience factor that has led to the immediate acceptance of the cash machine. There are several kinds of convenience factors, including *location* convenience. Self-service gas stations demonstrate the result of converging trends. Many of these stations serve only one automotive purpose: gasoline. They do not provide windshield cleaning, tire repair, battery charging or tune-ups. They have gotten out of the repair business. Many of those same service stations that used to raise cars up on hoists have turned into minimarts. Customers who stop to put gas in their own cars can also run inside for milk, bread, beer or other items. The gas station is offering location convenience to the driver. This kind of combined-purpose station will flourish in coming years because of the convenience.

Location convenience obviously is not a new concept. Newsstands at train stations, fast food outlets in shopping malls and hot-pretzel carts on Manhattan streets are all early examples of location convenience. What is happening now, however, is that marketers realize that the American appetite for convenience is growing. The market for such services should also grow.

The Value of Time

Another convenience factor is *time* convenience. Americans, especially urban Americans, are placing a greater value on their time. Life has become increasingly complicated because of the multiplicity of products, services, leisure activities and everything else that is available to us. In large cities workers are living farther away from their jobs and spending more time going to and from work. Market researchers say that the amount of leisure time enjoyed by the average adult has declined precipitously, from about 26 hours a week in the mid-1970s to 16 hours a week in the 1980s. People work more, exercise more, travel more. They have less time to watch television. The two-income household, mentioned frequently in this book, once again has a great bearing on time. Although we discuss family life and working mothers more fully in another chapter, we must also mention here that the two-income trend is enhancing the value of time convenience in our society. It is the primary reason for the rapid growth in recent years of the takeout food business. For many working mothers there simply isn't enough time to cook dinner every night. In the old days women cooked dinner six nights a week and were treated to dinner at a restaurant or carryout on the seventh night. In the future, families will eat out or carry in prepared foods five nights a week. Their weekend treat will be a homecooked meal. Time convenience is the only factor behind the ready acceptance of microwave ovens into American households. With 70% of the homes already equipped with a microwave, this appliance might well hold the speed record for penetrating the market.

The VCR is another item that has grown on its merits of time convenience. It has freed consumers from time constraints imposed by television programmers. If you can't watch a show while it is being telecast you can record it and play it back any time you want to. Or you can rent any movie and schedule show time for 8 P.M., midnight or 5 A.M.

Who can question the enormous success of facsimile transmission machines in American offices? Fax machines are being installed in hotel lobbies for guest use (for the price of a telephone call); by the end of the next decade, most American homes will have a telephone with a fax machine attached to it.

The whole convenience store industry was built on the basis of saving time for consumers. The larger supermarkets become, the more need there is for stores where customers can pop in for a few minutes and buy a couple of items. They are even willing to pay a little more for those items if it can save them some time. Some supermarkets are responding to the time demands by offering prepared foods such as hot soups, roasted chicken, salad bars and deli platters. The shopper might spend more time in the store but can save time by not having to cook dinner.

Time convenience is a powerful marketing tool. Its effects can be seen in the proliferation of one-day cleaners, six-hour photo processors, three-minute car washes, instant printers, express checkouts at hotels and express check-ins at car rental offices. Our younger generation has become so accustomed to this fast-forward service that they have developed a roaring demand for instant gratification in virtually every field. When they order a hamburger they expect to get it in one minute. Can you imagine their frustration if they were projected back into the 1950s and actually had to wait while the burger was being grilled? Today, speed is the key factor; it's the reason most of the fast-food chains have gotten even faster by offering drivethrough service.

In our quest to jam more experiences into our lives we will continue to demand products and services that can save us time. One big winner for the 1990s is expected to be liquid nitrogen–freezing technology for foods. The process freezes foods instantly, making them ideal for microwave cooking.

Making It Easy

The third important convenience factor is *effort* (or hassle) convenience. Anything that makes our lives less complicated will have a strong buyer appeal on the market. One of the hottest businesses of the 1980s was Domino's Pizza, not because the product was so superior but because the company delivered a hot pizza to your home or office within 30 minutes. This offered both effort convenience *and* time convenience.

The concept of catalog shopping exploded during the 1980s because it saved consumers the trouble of going out to stores. Research indicates that 51% of all adults in the United States ordered some merchandise by mail in the past year. The concept may have expanded too much, however, resulting in a tremendous amount of mail clutter in the average American home. Despite their names, most of the mail-order operations emphasized ordering by telephone, which reduced the hassle of mailing forms back and forth and also the amount of time needed to fulfill an order.

The ultimate in effortless shopping is buying via television, which registered a spotty record in its first few years. The basic problem with the concept as it was introduced was that often the wrong kinds of goods were being offered. Consumers want to save effort, but they also want to know what they are getting. Teleshopping will work when television or cable stations offer well-known brand-name items, especially merchandise that is purchased routinely, such as canned food, basic clothing and other staples. Any service that offers to deliver a product to the home will have a competitive edge in the 1990s. This even applies to traditional outlets such as pharmacies, liquor stores and grocery stores. The next step in video rental will be to call the store and have them beam a movie directly to your television set via airwave or telephone. Also look for rent-by-mail videotapes to be offered in the coming decade. We also expect there will be a significant increase in shopping via computer and telephone modem by the middle of the 1990s.

No matter what specific medium is used to move goods from the retailer to the consumer, we should anticipate that shopping at home will grow at an above-average rate. One ripe market for new business services in the next decade will be anything that can eliminate complexity from our lives. This is another reason why we see household managers and personal consultants fitting into our future. Consumers will also be looking for someone to take the hassle out of shopping for cars, buying insurance, arranging for health care, dealing with problem children (or even gifted children), and performing virtually any service that will take some of the clutter out of their busy lives.

FUTURE SCOPE

—————— ADVISORY ——————

Trends

- Consumer tastes are changing constantly as Americans respond quickly to fads and fashions. They are more likely to experiment with new products.

- Brand loyalty is staging a comeback, and generic products are disappearing from retail shelves.

- Americans are more quality-conscious. Perceived product value will become more important as population ages in the next decade.

- Because of technology and labor cost, Americans are getting less personal service than in earlier years. This will create an even greater demand for such services in the future.

- Busy Americans will respond to services and products that are convenient, speedy and effortless.

Strategies

- Market research and quick response time are crucial to any company in the consumer products field.

- Companies should stress the building of brands, concentrating on quality, confidence and value.

- The biggest opportunities will come for those who offer time-saving services to two-earner households. Consumers will be willing to pay more for services that save them time.

- Retailers should offer additional services such as takeout, drivethrough windows, home and office delivery and gift wrapping.

It's Almost 2000 *A.D.;* Do You Know Where Your Customers Are?

For the first couple of decades after World War II American consumers did exactly as the marketing theorists thought they would: They started living out their own real-life versions of "Ozzie and Harriet." These parents of the Baby Boom generation finished their high school or college education, married someone they went to school with, and settled down to start a family. The typical consumer bought a Ford or a Chevrolet station wagon, and when they accumulated enough money they put a down payment on a modest home in the suburbs. Typically, they made their weekly Saturday pilgrimage to the nearby shopping center. Of course, they visited Sears, Roebuck where they bought a set of screwdrivers, a lawn mower, a bag of fertilizer or a three-speed bicycle. Then they drove their station wagons over to a different shopping center for draperies, pajamas for the kids and a throw rug at J. C. Penney. Later that day Dad, caught up in the spirit of the do-it-yourself movement, would finish paneling the basement walls (he's turning it into a rec room) while Mom made a batch of cookies for Sissy's dance class and sewed achievement badges on Junior's Cub Scout uniform. After the chores were done Dad would mix a shaker of martinis for Mom and himself while she put the beef roast, vegetable casserole and apple pie into the oven. After a filling meal Mom and Dad would enjoy a cigarette together before tackling the dishes. A little bit later, exhausted by the full day of activities, they would collapse in front of the television set and enjoy the antics of Sid Caesar and Imogene Coca on "Your Show of Shows."

It was a little bit of middle class paradise. And pretty much the same thing happens today – with a few exceptions: Young couples get married five or six years later than their parents did. And they don't exactly leap into matrimony; they probably live together for a couple of years before making the big decision. They have a far more difficult time scraping together the down payment for a house. They still buy cars but not as many Fords and Chevrolets as they used to. They are more likely to start out with a Toyota or Nissan, then graduate up to a BMW or Volvo. They also don't shop at Sears and Penney's as much as the older generation, and they don't do-it-themselves anywhere near the extent that their parents did. They spend a good deal of their Saturdays getting bids from tradesmen for those little jobs around the house. They don't need a lawn mower because they have yard service, and they have stopped buying fertilizer because ChemLawn is so much more convenient. Mom doesn't do much sewing and cooking anymore because she works during the week and prefers to devote a few hours to herself on Saturdays. This usually includes an exercise session with her personal trainer, a jaunt on her 18-speed mountain bike and, of course, a visit to the analyst. They also don't eat very much beef anymore; nor do they drink liquor – except for an occasional glass of white wine. They stopped smoking ten years ago (even marijuana). If they do stay home for dinner on a Saturday night, which is rare, they never watch television; they don't even know what's on. Their favorite relaxation is to rent a movie and pop it into the VCR. One reason life has changed so dramatically for this modern-day suburban family is because they have only one child; or maybe they don't have any.

These two scenarios obviously are stereotypes, but that doesn't mean they aren't fairly accurate representations of a substantial proportion of American families. And the changes in lifestyle enumerated in the latter example can all be borne out by actual statistics.

These changes were crucial to the business world in that they signaled the emergence of a new American consumer. But the changes still befuddled marketing experts at many consumer products companies and retailers who failed to recognize that Americans were going through a major transition in the late 1970s and 1980s, when the Baby Boomers were just coming of age. Hundreds of companies went out of business or lost significant market share because they weren't prepared for how American buying patterns would shift. The same dangers exist for today's marketers who don't bother to peek into the future.

Because the field of consumer preference is so vast, we will concentrate on a couple of important trends that have persisted for several years and apparently will continue for the next decade and perhaps longer.

Finding the Niche

One of the overriding trends of recent years has been the growing importance of specialization—finding a niche in the marketplace and then filling that niche with the appropriate product or service. What marketers have found in recent years is that no niche is too small. In fact, the smaller the niche, the stronger the attraction for customers. If you look back at recent history you can see that we spent the first half of this century building huge enterprises. Big was beautiful. General Motors is an example of a giant company formed by the amalgamation of several smaller companies. It grew into the largest auto manufacturing company in the world but then was beset by smaller companies who took away great chunks of market share. Sears, Roebuck expanded into the largest retailer in the world—it still is—but it is nowhere near having the market clout today that it had 20 years ago. It is a company that has run into trouble and is on the brink of momentous change. *Life* magazine is a good example of a publication that became an institution in the United States. Its great prose and dramatic photojournalism set it apart from any other magazine ever published. At its peak *Life* was going into eight million American homes every week. Then one day *Life* was gone. Bigness does not guarantee success.

Publishing, in fact communications as a whole, may well provide the best example of how market segmentation or specialization has taken over an industry. We can see why *Life* ran out its string by taking a brief look at the history of communications. As recently as 70 years ago mass communications as we know it did not exist.

Perhaps the most powerful media at the time were national magazines and daily newspapers, but their circulations were limited. After all, who was educated enough to read in those years? At the turn of the century, 12% of all Americans were totally illiterate, and a far higher percentage were functionally illiterate. They might have been able to sign their names, but that was it. In addition, we were awash in immigrants who couldn't speak or read English. We started the decade of 1900–10 with a population of 75 million, and during the decade 8.8 million immigrants arrived here, adding more than 10% to our population. Our mass communications capabilities in those years were no more advanced than smoke signals or jungle drums. Word of mouth was probably the most universal form of communications at the time, not unlike the town criers of old who rang their bells, made their announcements, then moved to another town square.

We can't identify any specific date for the beginning of mass communications, but we like to place it in the fall of 1927. The New York Yankees were playing the Pittsburgh Pirates in the World Series. More important for our purposes, this was the first series that was broadcast from coast to coast on a new medium called radio. (The Yankees, of course, won the series in four straight games.) It marked the first time that thousands of Americans across the country joined together simultaneously to be earwitnesses to a national event described to them. That primitive broadcast was the progenitor of what has developed into a major industry and a remarkable national pastime, televised sports, best symbolized today by the gaudy excesses of the Super Bowl telecasts.

Within a decade after this first nationwide radio event, mass communications came into its own, and radio became the key element. It eventually induced millions of families to sit down in front of the radio set every night and be entertained by a dazzling array of programming: detective programs, situation comedies, cowboy serials, quiz shows, soap operas, news and commentary programs, variety shows, sports, ballroom dance music and all of the rest. In that same era the great newsweeklies started to flourish: *Life, Time, Newsweek, Look, Saturday Evening Post, Reader's Digest* and others were growing gigantic circulations. Newspapers, although many were started in the nineteenth century, didn't really reach mass audiences until the 1930s. The coming of war in the 1940s pushed all of mass communications ahead. Americans were hungry for news from over-seas. They wanted to soak up every shred of information about the war that had separated them from their sons and husbands and fathers.

The Mass Media Champ

The principal media continued to be radio, newspapers and *Life* magazine, but Americans got their most vivid images of overseas through the movie newsreels. These film snippets of news from the front whetted their appetites for a new means of communication that was yet to happen. Only after the war did this revolutionary new medium — television — burst into the American consciousness. Whatever we thought mass communications was before then was redefined by television, which had the sound of radio and pictures that were better than *Life*'s because they moved. Television was superior to newsreels because it was live and immediate. None of the other media could compete with that combination.

In 1947 there were ten television stations operating across the country and 160,000 television sets in the market. By the end of 1948 there were 128 television stations in operation. In 1950 alone 7.5 million television sets were sold, penetrating nearly 20% of the households in the country in only one year. The advent of television marked a major transition that should have been expected in the communications industry. The technology had been developed in the 1930s. The only reason it wasn't deployed sooner was because of the war. Even with all of this warning, radio was still nearly devastated by television. The medium born in the 1920s virtually died in the 1950s as its programs and major advertisers shifted en masse to television.

Stripped of its top shows and personalities, radio resorted to the cheapest programming available. It started playing phonograph records on the air. The medium that had stunningly informed us of the bombing of Pearl Harbor with Walter Cronkite describing the horrors of war; the medium that made stars of Jack Benny, Bob Hope, George Burns, Orson Welles and hundreds of others, was reduced to being nothing more than a glorified jukebox. Television had other victims, too. It nearly delivered a deathblow to the movie industry. Within two years more than half the country's movie theaters closed their doors. People could watch all kinds of programs, including old

164

movies, for free in their homes. Why did they have to go to the movie houses anymore?

Magazines also felt the chill of television's influence. As long-time magazine advertisers started shifting much of their revenues into television, the magazines started to go out of business. The list of casualties included some of the biggest and most powerful publications in the country: *Life, Look, Saturday Evening Post, Collier's, Coronet, Pageant* and many others. The 1950s and 1960s also saw dozens of major metropolitan newspapers print their final editions. Some of them were newspapers with great journalistic heritages, like the *New York Herald Tribune* and the *Chicago Daily News.* Most were evening newspapers that had lost readers and advertisers to television.

Television had become the undisputed grand champion of mass communications. And yet, when we look at the communications industry today we can readily see that radio has not died; indeed it is healthier than ever before. The magazine industry also has been riding high. These media have thrived because they were forced to do something that was antithetical to the evolution of mass communications: Rather than blindly chase after bigger audiences they specialized in segmented audiences. The difference in the way we listen to radio makes that point eloquently. Back in the 1930s and 1940s, families gathered together in front of the radio in the evenings and listened to programming that was created largely for the whole family. Today the family listens to radio from wake-up time (clock radios) to bedtime, but we don't listen together. We are all plugged into those Walkman-type portables listening to our own programs or listening in our cars as we negotiate rush-hour traffic on our way to work.

Rather than offering a few programs aimed at mass audiences, radio today is a personal medium with a wide range of specific formats for different segments of the market. In any major metropolitan area, the range of formats will include all-talk, all-news, classical, beautiful music, religious, disco, rap music and up to a dozen varieties of rock, each aimed at a specific demographic and psychographic segment. The same has happened in magazine publishing. General interest mass-circulation publications are virtually extinct. National magazines have been replaced by an army of regional and metropolitan "lifestyle" publications, such as *Los Angeles* magazine and *Southern*

Living. Being regional is a basic form of market segmentation because you appeal to people who live in a defined area.

Targeting Women

Another form of segmentation is demonstrated by the women's magazine field. A couple of decades ago, women's magazines fell into two categories. One category was made up of service books, such as *Good Housekeeping* and *Ladies' Home Journal,* which competed on the basis of which had the best meat-loaf recipe of the month. The other category consisted of fashion magazines *(Vogue, Mademoiselle)* displaying an array of apparel that only a stick figure could wear. When *Ms.* magazine started in 1973 it appealed to a woman as someone other than a housewife or fashion hound. It appealed to a psychographic segment of the audience that was more interested in personal fulfillment and equal opportunity. The market has since been splintered into even smaller shards, and the titles tell exactly at whom the publications are aimed: *Working Woman, Working Mother, New York Woman, Today's Chicago Woman.* There is also *Savvy Woman* magazine for the woman executive and *Lear's* "for the woman who wasn't born yesterday."

There also has been an explosion in special-interest publications aimed at specific audiences, from bodybuilders to needlepointers. One new entry is *Tan* magazine, aimed at tanning salon patrons. One of the most successful categories of special-interest magazines are in-flight publications supplied by the airlines. Advertisers choose these magazines not only because airline travelers tend to have good demographics for advertisers but also because they know exactly where the readers are when they are looking through them. They are flying on airplanes and reading the magazines because they have time to kill. Another publisher trying to capitalize on this same factor was an entrepreneur in Cleveland who a couple of years ago started a magazine called *Bathroom Journal.* He also could tell advertisers exactly where his magazine was being read—and could guarantee that he had a captive audience. But because everyone uses a bathroom every now and then, this publication wasn't specialized enough . . . and went down the drain.

In addition to about 3,500 consumer publications of all kinds, there also are some 10,000 trade publications aimed at virtually every business and occupation. In the past 20 years alone, hundreds of computer magazines have been established, with each successive one chopping off smaller, more specialized segments of the market. Today virtually every popular piece of hardware and software has a publication devoted exclusively to it.

Back in 1979, the *Wall Street Journal* was undisputed leader among business publications, with a nationwide audience of two million readers. That was the year in which the Association of Area Business Publications was formed, initially with a dozen members and combined circulation of less than 200,000. These business publications are aimed at specific markets and range from the largest in the field, *Crain's Chicago Business,* down to medium-size newspapers like the *Phoenix Business Journal* and much smaller ones such as the *Grand Rapids Business Journal.* Today the association has nearly 100 members and a combined circulation of 2.25 million. The *Wall Street Journal*'s circulation has since dropped to less than 1.9 million, and its advertising lineage has declined by an even larger share.

Even though television still reigns supreme in the arena of mass communications, it also is being affected by the movement toward specialization and segmentation. The prime-time network audience has been shrinking steadily over the past 20 years from 90% to 70%, and in recent surveys to little more than 60%. Once again, the audience is shunning national mass programming in favor of programming more specific to their needs and tastes. There has been a concurrent growth in viewing levels of local independent stations and cable television. In 1988, 54% of the households in the country were hooked to cable, up from only 7.5% in 1970. The penetration is moving up two to three percentage points a year.

Also taking a big bite out of the network audience is something that might be the epitome of specialization: the videocassette recorder and player. Viewers can choose any movie they want to see and can watch it any time that's convenient for them. They don't have to wait for a television station or cable channel to put it on the air. By the end of the 1980s, movie rentals from video stores were running at about 2.3 billion a year. This is nearly double the total number of books, records, films, pamphlets and videos that are circulated by all of the public libraries in the United States. This unprecedented demand for home entertainment will create a tremendous market for more movies and any other feature that is appropriate fare for a VCR. The movie exhibition industry, which was leveled by television 40 years ago, will face the same danger in the 1990s.

Although there will always be some demand for entertainment out-side the home, many others — especially the elderly — prefer to watch a movie in the comfort of their homes. Theaters aren't a necessary element in the distribution of a movie to the public. Years ago tele-vision started producing its own movies-of-the-week. More recently, cable programmers such as Home Box Office have also produced motion pictures to be played only on cable. In the future, movies also will be produced specifically for videocassette distribution.

In late 1988 the last movie theater in downtown Chicago closed its doors. That city's Loop, which once dazzled with millions of twinkling marquee lights from a score of huge theaters, was without a major screen for the first time in 75 years. They were replaced by dozens of smaller theaters tucked away in shopping malls and trendy neighborhoods. This is another form of market segmentation, multiple small screens instead of one large theater. But even many of these will flicker out, leaving only a few healthy theaters by thc end of the 1990s.

Segmenting the Media

The trend toward more specialized and segmented media is likely to continue in the next decade. One basic reason is because major advertisers have started shifting their dollars toward new outlets such as cable television. The criterion for an advertising medium is no longer how big its audience is but how well it covers the demographic or psychographic group the advertiser is trying to reach. This erosion of mass media isn't a new idea. It is one aspect of the "de-massified society" that Alvin Toffler identified in his seminal work, *The Third Wave,* written in 1980.

As the targeting of media expands in the next decade the results will be seen in various ways. Laser printing will allow publications to personalize advertisements. Advertisements in magazines can be personalized to contain the name of the person to whom the subscrip-tion is mailed. Magazines will increase their number of special editions, offering not only geographical breakouts but other special demographic breakouts based on the age, sex, race or occupation of their readers. *Newsweek* magazine, for example, could attract more advertising directed at women if it created a special section or edition that went only to female subscribers.

Newspapers will move more heavily into zoned editions, trying to compete with the rapidly growing suburban press. Newspapers, by the way, are the only major medium that has resisted segmentation, which is the reason they are still suffering from the impact of television.

Videotext will finally happen in the 1990s. This is a system whereby subscribers use their personal computers to tap into a daily data base, getting everything from news headlines to baseball scores and stock prices. Even though many major companies experimented with the concept in the 1980s, it flopped. We predict that it will be established within the next decade, but it will be a highly selective service aimed only at the most affluent segment of the market. It will be expensive but worth the price to those who want instant access to news and information. The concept didn't work previously because it was influenced by newspaper people who, failing to grasp the principle of segmentation, thought they could snare the mass market.

Slicing the Retail Pie

This same trend toward specializaton has started dominating many areas of business; retailing is a perfect example. Over the past ten years American shoppers have seen many major department store chains go out of business. At the same time, national full-service retailers such as Sears, Montgomery Ward and J. C. Penney have all experienced slow growth or no growth. And they have had trouble maintaining their customer base. But specialty stores are booming. Customers seek out retailers that specialize in sporting goods, toys, jewelry, crafts, electronics, records, auto parts and such. Some of these retail outlets have developed into what the industry calls "category killers," outlets that carry a huge selection of items, such as Toys R Us or Builders Square. Anyone about to do some serious toy shopping is more likely to go to a store that has a tremendous selection of toys, plus good prices, rather than go to a department store with only a limited choice of items.

What is interesting is that the specialty stores are developing sub-specialties. Foot Locker, a chain of stores selling only athletic shoes — a fairly narrow niche — has developed another chain called Lady Foot Locker, athletic shoes for women only. There are Gap jeans stores, but also Gap for Kids. The Italian-based Benetton chain has outlets strictly for school-age children. In men's clothing, department stores that offer all things to all men are losing customers to boutique-type haberdashers that specialize in a particular style of clothes, such as British, Italian or American fashions. Some outlets even specialize in specific designers, such as Giorgio Armani, Calvin Klein or Ungaro.

The plight of general merchandise retailers was illustrated in 1989, when Chas. A. Stevens, a 103-year-old Chicago department store chain for women, went out of business. "The big department store as a women's specialty emporium doesn't appear to have a place in today's market," Stevens president, John W. Lee, was quoted as saying. "The idea is to go small and focused, and we were trying to do it in a big store environment."

We apparently have not reached the limit as to how narrow a retail niche can be. How about a chain of stores, such as Mrs. Field's, that sells only cookies? (Cookies!) The chain even ran into some problems in 1988 when it tried to expand into muffins.

Speaking of food, the same kind of specialization has found its way into the restaurant business. Many of the old-fashioned, family-run eclectic restaurants have fallen by the wayside. Taking over the business have been legions of restaurants that specialize in a specific cuisine or even a specific dish. McDonald's would have never grown into the world's largest restaurant chain if it had offered a full menu of dishes. The same goes for Kentucky Fried Chicken, Red Lobster, Arby's, Dunkin' Donuts and Taco Bell. This same trend toward specialization has spread to numerous areas of business and even the professions, such as health care. Various specialty centers have opened that treat very specific problems, such as hernias, hemorrhoids, varicose veins or sports injuries. This is only a reflection of how the old general practitioner has been outnumbered by specialists in recent years. This trend will continue to expand in medicine and will also grow in law, where attorneys increasingly will specialize in narrow niches of practice such as divorce, traffic violations, age discrimination, sexual harassment and drug charges. Some forms of specialization have long existed in the legal business, but they will expand because the number of lawyers per capita has grown quite steadily. Competition among lawyers will grow far more intense in the next decade, and law firms will gradually adopt more formal marketing programs, including public relations and advertising.

Law, like medicine, is years behind other businesses. Rather than regionalize, the trend in law is to go national, with firms merging or setting up new offices in key markets across the country. We expect, however, that clients will tend to look for specialists in the future. Developing specialities will produce a stronger marketing position than having no particular area of expertise. This is more applicable to individual lawyers and small firms than to firms that are large enough to develop their own special practices. The same theory of specialization can be applied to virtually any business, especially small businesses that can't seem to compete against larger full-service competitors. In many cases the way to survive, and even thrive, is to specialize in one particular segment, category or subcategory. The toy store, for example, that is losing customers to a major toy "category killer" might find a market if it specialized in educational toys, preschool items, handmade goods, ethnic dolls, electronic toys, learning games or such.

Market Bifurcation:
Adding to the Specialty Trend

Another gradual change that has occurred in American buying patterns over the past two decades has been what observers have called the bifurcation or polarization of product markets. This is somewhat related to the specialization trend described in the previous section. This polarization exists in any category of products in which there is an increase in buying at the high-price and the low-price ends of the market. It is accompanied by a defection of customers away from the mid-priced, moderate-quality goods. In the retail field, for example, the most consistent growth over the past 20 years has taken place in two prime areas: upscale retailers and rock bottom–priced outlets.

High-priced retailers such as Nieman-Marcus, Bloomingdale's, Gucci, Ralph Lauren, Burberry's and others have spread from their home bases to many other parts of the country. They are taking a larger share of the retail dollar and probably will continue to do so in the coming years. At the other end of the spectrum are the price cutters, starting with discounters such as K mart, which has grown into the nation's second largest retailer, close on the heels of Sears. But the low end of the market has a wide variety of off-price operations, and there seems to be no limit to the range of options. Some are general retailers with national chains, such as T. J. Maxx, which sells overstocked inventories and irregular merchandise. Customers in record numbers are resisting the idea of paying list price for anything. Anyone who says "I can get it for you wholesale" is attracting the attention of shoppers.

The off-price concept accelerated in the mid-1980s with the establishment of whole shopping centers made up exclusively of factory outlet stores for clothing, household items, office products and virtually anything else that can be sold at retail. We see the concept expanding in the next decade because the shopping public is getting older, and older customers are more likely to patronize off-price stores.

While the discounters have been grabbing a larger share of the retail business, dozens of middle-market retailers in many cities have fallen by the wayside. The list of retail tombstones includes Gimbel's of New York, Wieboldt's of Chicago, Lit Brothers of Philadelphia, J. L. Hudson of Detroit and the W. T. Grant national chain—all examples of mid-priced retailers that could not compete. The combination of upscale-downscale competition lured away too many customers. This is the same problem that has faced Sears and Montgomery Ward. It is only their sheer size that has allowed them to withstand the heavy competition, especially from discounters. The two chains responded to the pressure in 1988 by adopting low-price concepts at their stores. At the time this book was being written, both of the huge retailers were also opening specialty stores for electronics, hardware, auto parts and other goods. The low-price and specialty concepts may well enhance the prospects of the two retailers and keep them viable through the 1990s. Another merchant that successfully repositioned itself out of the middle of the market was

Spiegel, the large catalog and outlet retailer. Rather than go the discount route the company upgraded its merchandise and acquired more of a fashion image in the late 1970s, which resulted in a classic sales turnaround.

Polarizing the Car Biz

Aside from retailing, the polarized market syndrome has also affected the American auto business for several years. Going back to the mid-1970s, Detroit ignored the fact that consumers were looking for something other than what they were producing, the standard or mid-size cars that were increasingly looking more and more alike. American automakers, like middle-of-the-road retailers, were being attacked on both sides of the price spectrum. As the fuel crisis deepened, small, low-priced and fuel-efficient cars were flowing into this country primarily from Japan. They captured the bottom of the market, with Toyota, Nissan, Mazda and Subaru becoming household names. Then the European invasion of high-priced, quality-made luxury cars skimmed off the top of the market—notably BMW, Saab, Mercedes-Benz, Volvo, Jaguar, Porsche. All registered tremendous sales increases during the 1980s. American cars did start to stage a comeback on both ends of the market after the dollar declined in the late 1980s, but by that time imports were claiming about 30% of the car market in the United States. At the same time the American carmakers were suffering from marketing myopia, the quality of cars coming off their assembly lines had deteriorated badly. It took several years of redesign, retooling, remarketing and public relations efforts before American cars started winning back a reputation for quality.

Polarization has also been evident in the nation's supermarkets for several years. The price sensitivity of the retail food business was demonstrated by the early success of generic products on the market. We also have seen the establishment of food discount chains as well as warehouse club operations in some parts of the country. But while this was happening there was a concurrent burst in the sale of gourmet food items. Americans bought generic paper towels to save 20 cents and then turned around and looked for special blends of Colombian coffee at nine dollars a pound. Gourmet or specialty foods make up the fastest-growing segment of the food market, which overall has had sluggish sales in the past few years.

Shreds of evidence of polarized buying can also be detected in the restaurant business, alcoholic beverages, airlines and lodging industry. The Marriott Hotel chain has responded to the trend by developing five different "brands" of hotels with different identities, all appealing to different segments of the markets.

Mysteries of the Marketplace

One wrong assumption to avoid is that poor people buy low-priced goods and affluent people buy high-priced ones; that isn't necessarily the case. A lot of rich people drive Toyotas while those of modest means might drive Cadillacs. And sometimes the same person will go high-end with one purchase and low-end with another. An example is the consumer who shells out $50,000 for a Mercedes-Benz, then shops at K mart to get a dollar off on a bag of lawn fertilizer. Is this unusual? Emphatically no. After all, there are more discount stores in affluent suburbs than in inner cities. Examples of high-low polarized buying can even be found when the same people are buying products in the same category. Here's a real-life example: A young couple is browsing through a large liquor store. The man is cradling a bottle of Chateau La Tour, a fine French wine that probably goes at $40 a bottle. His female companion, meanwhile, has a firm grip on a jug of Gallo Hearty Burgundy, which is about one-fifth the price. Does this make sense? It certainly does if you understand why the couple is making these purchases. They are going to take the good wine as a gift when they go to a friend's home for a celebration dinner. The other stuff they will enjoy in the privacy of their own home. There is no mystery behind their actions; they are actually buying different goods for different purposes. The same range of buying motivations applies to autos. Some people buy for transportation; others buy for status. The challenge is to find out what will prompt customers to buy particular products.

This is an ideal time to marry together the two changes we have explored up to now: specialization and polarization. They really have a direct relationship because polarization is a form of specialization. Providing the highest priced and highest quality of any product category is a special niche in itself. That provides potential customers with a very compelling reason to buy the item. At the same time, having the most economical product in a category is also a strong niche. Of all the niches, in fact, these two might provide the clearest motivations for any potential customer.

In order to reiterate the importance of specialization, let's look back at the automotive market one more time. In addition to sales at the top and the bottom of the category we can also see that many other automotive categories have grown in recent years. These include sports cars, four-wheel-drive vehicles, vans, small trucks and convertibles. Most of these are priced in the middle of the market, but each of these is a specialty vehicle, as opposed to the standard, all-purpose sedans that fill no niche in the market and have plummeted in sales in the past 20 years.

There is only one outlook for the future: more of the same. One reason that product differentiation is so important is because of the multiplicity of products on the market. Our options are increasing very steadily and will continue to increase in most areas. This is true for cars, magazines, shampoos, breakfast cereals and many other categories.

Several surveys have indicated that consumers are often confused by the proliferation of competing brands, flavors, colors, sizes, strengths and variations of products on the market. We are at a point now where virtually no sane American knows exactly what any specific cold remedy is supposed to do for any specific part of the body. The reason that specialization and polarization are not as important in other countries—yet—is because Americans have more product offerings than any other society in the world.

The marketing champion of the next decade will be the person who can develop a sense of "nichemanship." This person will be able to identify target markets, determine their specific needs and produce goods that will fill those needs. Products that don't fill those specific needs will not attract the attention of shoppers confronted with a multitude of brands. Because of this there is no question that marketing will be one of the key disciplines of the next decade, not only to sell products to consumers but primarily to find out what consumers want out of a product.

The increased use of the computer, as well as more refined data, will push marketers more deeply into segmented marketing. This is one reason that rifle-shot techniques such as direct mail and telemarketing have been snaring a larger share of the dollars that previously went into mass advertising. More than 60 billion pieces of third-class mail moved through the U.S. Postal Service in 1987, the vast majority of it trying to sell us something. Those who sell by mail or solicit charitable contributions will pay up to ten cents or more for the name and address of a potential prospect. Once you buy from a direct mail catalog your name will be added to a list of active buyers, and you can expect a torrent of catalogs from all kinds of merchandisers.

The hottest targeting technique of the 1990s will be telemarketing. The calls are annoying to many of the people who receive them, but many marketers say the response is better than other forms of advertising. This is the next decade's reincarnation of the old-fashioned door-to-door salesperson.

The next decade will see even more targeting, based on media that range from fax machines to home computers to interactive cable television. Another reason the specialization-polarization trends will flourish may well be what some researchers believe is a movement toward "component lifestyles."

Americans—especially the affluent ones—are independent and are blessed (or cursed) with a multitude of options regarding virtually everything; they don't have to fit into a fairly rigid lifestyle. In other words, they don't have to buy the whole package. You can wear a fancy mink coat but still buy your underwear at K mart. You can grab a quick lunch at McDonald's and linger over dinner at Lutéce—all in the same day.

Companies selling consumer goods will have to discard much of the broadscale demographic background for their marketing plans and rely on much smaller circles of consumer behavior. They also will have to learn how to appeal to the individualism of the affluent, which no doubt will filter down to those of more modest means.

FUTURE SCOPE

Trends

- Family lifestyles are changing because of two-income households and fewer children.

- Consumers are tending away from general merchandise marketers and toward retailers that specialize in particular products.

- They also are shifting away from mass media, such as network television and newspapers, to segmented media, such as specialized publications and cable television.

- Markets are becoming polarized, with customers shifting to the high end and low end and moving away from middle-of-the-road options.

Strategies

- Consumer companies must study trends to track demands being made by the new kind of families of the 1990s.

- Marketers and merchandisers should develop products and services that fill specific niches and subniches in the market.

- Advertisers must emphasize media targeted at specific audiences and use mass media only if products are aimed at the mass market.

- Businesses must develop pricing strategies and identify specific product features to avoid being caught in the declining middle of the market.

CHAPTER 12

A Generation of Fitness Fanatics

The way Americans have been taking care of themselves lately, you might think they plan on living forever. They obviously won't do that, but they will, on the average, live longer than any other generation of their predecessors. Medical advances play an important part in this extended longevity, but some credit must also go to better nutrition, avoidance of harmful foods, a reduction in cigarette smoking and an increase in regular exercise programs. Twenty years ago, when the pioneer fitness fanatics started jogging, and early health foods stores opened their doors, a lot of critics considered the spurt of interest in fitness to be just another fad. At the same time others were saying that rock music was just a fad. All these years later, both fads are still booming, although one is much louder than the other. The quieter one, the fitness fad, has developed into a trend that will affect the lives of generations to come. Not everybody is participating in this trend. There are still those who eat like trenchermen and avoid exercise at all costs. Many Americans still smoke cigarettes even knowing the habit leads to cancer and other respiratory diseases. Others take illegal drugs or drink too much alcohol. Still others drive recklessly or refuse to wear life-saving seatbelts. In the late 1980s the "couch potato" phenomenon erupted as a revolution against the fitness trend. But by all indications, it is the sofa spuds who are part of a mere fad.

Health consciousness—in its various manifestations—has grown steadily over the past 20 years. Participation in individual sports activities might rise or fall, based on many variables. Various kinds of health foods and vitamins may go in and out of vogue, but the desire on the part of Americans to be healthier and fitter will not fade in the next decade. There is a very good reason for this trend to continue indefinitely. We know more about our bodies than any earlier generation. We have better diagnostic tools and a finer understanding of nutrition. For reasons we will point out later in the chapter, this trend will expand in the 1990s.

This is not to say that healthful living is a new pursuit. For many years, Americans were obsessed with at least one aspect of fitness: losing weight. At the heart of the obsession was the fact, of course, that we eat too much and thus weigh too much. What has gradually changed over the years, though, is our motivation for losing weight. Twenty years ago the principal reason most people went on diets was to look good. Increasingly, however, health concerns have become an important element in motivating people to monitor and limit their intake of food.

A growing percentage of the adult American population say that they are "watching what they eat." A national survey conducted in 1987 by *Prevention* magazine disclosed that 44% of the women and 31% of the men surveyed said that they were on diets. A good number of these people were not dieting to fit into a new bikini but were addressing concerns of high blood pressure, high cholesterol or other ailments. Still others, adopting a more healthful diet as a preventive measure, eat less fat, more fiber and more carbohydrates. All of this is evident in the development of diets over the years. Back in the postwar days crash diets were the rage, and we saw every form of screwball diet imaginable. People went on grapefruit diets, liquid protein diets, all-beef diets, even the so-called drinking man's diet. The tone of diets started shifting as we moved into the 1980s. Health became more important than quick, cosmetic weight loss. We became conscious not only of low-calorie but low-sodium diets, low-cholesterol diets and high-fiber diets. The burgeoning demand for fiber in the past decade is one example of how eager Americans are to eat themselves into good shape. Several landmark studies have indicated that a high-fiber diet can lessen chances of developing colon cancer, a major killer. As this word spread to the general public, sales of high-fiber products soared. Today we eat so much high-fiber breakfast cereals it's a wonder we make it from home to the office without a pit stop on the way.

In the midst of the fiber boom, additional studies indicated that oat bran was a better source of fiber than other types of bran; it even reportedly could help lower cholesterol levels. That was all consumers had to hear. Oat bran was so much in demand that supermarkets had trouble keeping the product on their shelves. Some food manufacturers said that for nearly a year they couldn't keep up with the demand.

Quaker Oats, one of the first companies to market oat bran products, said that 1988 sales of the cereal were seven times higher than in 1987. Even the names manufacturers gave to their oat bran products suggested that these were a different ilk — not Fruit Loops or Cap'n Crunch. General Mills's oat bran cereal was named Benefit, while Kellogg's was called Common Sense.

Whether the fiber demand or the oat bran craze will expand over the next decade is difficult to assess at this point. If research continues to indicate that high-fiber diets can reduce a person's chances of contracting colon cancer and provide other health benefits, then we can expect demand for fiber to increase. In addition to cereals, we are likely to see other products fortified with fiber. We are, after all, a little nutsy about magic cures. We are very likely to overindulge in fiber in the same way many of us consume far more than the adult daily requirement of vitamins. The fact that our population will gradually be getting older throughout the 1990s also indicates that demand for high-fiber and other nutritional products will increase.

There is still a good deal of controversy over the need for supplemental vitamins and minerals for anyone who follows a well-balanced regimen. Nevertheless, an increasing number of Americans spend a bundle of money on vitamins; estimates exceeded three billion dollars a year in the late 1980s. It may well turn out that some of the demand spikes for specific nutritional supplements will end up as fads. Americans started megadosing on Vitamin C when Dr. Linus Pauling said that it could prevent or minimize the symptoms of the common cold. We added Vitamin E to our diets when someone suggested that it could help our sexual performance. We demanded fish oil when we learned it could improve our cholesterol levels.

But even if some of these specific instances turn out to be fads, it doesn't take away from the long-term trend, which indicates that we are more interested in good nutrition than any earlier generation. The demand for supplemental vitamins is so strong it has prompted many food companies to fortify their products with various vitamins and minerals. These nutritional boosters can be found in a wide array of items, from breakfast cereals to fruit juices and snacks. A couple of years back, even the makers of Tums antacid tablets and Tab diet cola promoted their products as being high in calcium, a mineral proven helpful in fighting osteoporosis.

America's Careful Eaters

Increased consumption of vitamin supplements is only the most visible aspect of the nutrition boom. There are other less obvious indicators of the trend toward health consciousness. One example is beef consumption. Despite the huge amount of business being done by McDonald's, Burger King, Wendy's and other hamburger chains, per-capita consumption of red meat has declined substantially in the United States since peaking in the mid-1970s. The primary reason is that animal fats have been accused of contributing to high cholesterol levels, which contribute to heart disease. Between 1975 and 1980, per-capita consumption of red meat declined by 13% in the United States. Consumption started edging upward in the late 1980s but is expected to dip again in the 1990s as the population ages. Consumption of veal, lamb and pork have also declined in recent years.

Another cholesterol villain—eggs—suffered an even worse slide, declining 9% in per-capita consumption since 1975 and 25% since 1960. Nutrition, of course, isn't the only reason—and perhaps isn't the main reason—that determines what products people buy. Price and availability are also key factors.

Butter is another cholesterol producer whose consumption has melted slowly, from 7.7 pounds per capita in 1960 to less than four pounds in the late 1980s. Margarine consumption gained modestly in that period, which makes us wonder what Americans are spreading on their morning toast. The butter industry has decided to fight back and budgeted $14 million for an advertising campaign in 1989.

For many Americans beef is still the primary entrée, but the slide in sales has been so ominous that the beef industry has spent millions of dollars on an advertising campaign to promote consumption of beef. This also may help win back some customers.

While red meat consumption was declining, Americans were increasing their appetite for foods generally considered more healthful. Between 1970 and 1986 per-capita chicken consumption was up 48%; fish consumption was up 25%; turkey consumption up 68%; fresh fruits up 18%; and fresh vegetables up 25%.

In the late 1980s nutritional experts identified the so-called tropical oils—coconut, palm and palm kernel—as extremely high in saturated fats, a leading cause of cholesterol. Consumer reaction was so negative that many major makers of cookies and crackers began reformulating their recipes, substituting polyunsaturated oils.

Nowhere is the nutritional motivation behind food selection more evident than in milk, where whole milk consumption dived by 45% in per-capita consumption while low-fat milk was soaring by 131%. With sugar consumption also declining by 40% you might think that all Americans should be as svelte as Cher; but they aren't.

There is little question that we are more careful about what we eat. Beverage consumption statistics show that we also are being just as careful in what we drink. Take coffee for example. Per-capita consumption of coffee, another commodity with negative health implications, is half of what it was in 1962. Back then, 75% of American adults were regular coffee drinkers, compared with only 50% today. Fewer people drink coffee, and those who do drink less. At the same time, the percentage of decaf drinkers has quadrupled, from 4% in 1962 to about 16% currently; and even a substantial percentage of regular caffeinated coffee drinkers switch to decaffeinated late in the day.

Two Troubled Industries

Because of improved nutritional practices, several major industries are facing bleak futures as we head toward the twenty-first century. Those hit the hardest probably will be cigarettes and alcoholic beverages. Breaking the cigarette habit has not been quick or easy for most smokers. But the numbers have been declining steadily since 1964, when the landmark U.S. Surgeon General's report on the health hazards of smoking was released. The percentage of adults who smoke cigarettes has dropped from 43% in 1974 to about 27% in recent years. What troubles health experts is that all of the decline has come among men smokers, while the percentage of women smokers has actually increased slightly. Despite the larger number of women smokers and the growing population, the total number of cigarettes sold peaked in 1981 and has slipped significantly since then. It will continue to dive because fewer young people are smoking. In 1974, 25% of those in the 12-to-17 age group were smokers (an astoundingly high percentage) compared with 15% today.

Health officials estimate that about one million young people start smoking every year, while 1.3 million smokers swear off. At this rate, nearly four-fifths of American adults will be nonsmokers by 2000. Not included in the projection are the hundreds of thousands of people who die every year from smoking-related causes.

There is a reverse correlation between cigarette smoking and education. Among college graduates only 18% are smokers, which is about half the percentage of smokers without a high school diploma. Among entering college freshmen in 1988 only 9% were smokers. As the percentage of Americans going to college increases, it will contribute to the decline in smoking. Also adding to the dim future of tobacco is a growing antismoking lobby of consumer activists and health experts. Many are average citizens tired of inhaling the smoke from other people's cigarettes. Their pressure has contributed to a federal smoking ban on airline flights of less than two hours and also to many state and local limitations on smoking in restaurants, workplaces and other public places.

A study conducted recently by the National Center for Health Statistics indicates that certain groups of people seem disposed toward a variety of unhealthy habits. Smokers, for example, are more likely to be heavy drinkers and nonexercisers. They also tend to get less sleep and are likelier to skip breakfast than nonsmokers are.

Alcoholic beverages are also facing some tough times ahead (the recent past hasn't been so great either). Sales of hard liquor peaked in 1983 and have declined every year since then. The greatest drop-off has been in what the industry calles "brown goods" — scotch, bourbon, rye and blended whiskies. Part of this has been perceived as the American public's swing to lighter tasting products such as vodka, rum and tequila. Back in the 1970s, several liquor companies tried to cater to this shift in taste by putting a significant marketing effort behind a new category called "light whisky." All of the products in the category bombed within a couple of years. It appears that the American appetite for alcohol is declining, regardless of taste.

Beer sales also peaked in per-capita consumption in 1983, and wine sales flattened out a couple of years later. One interesting note in the beer market is that sales would have slumped tremendously if it weren't for the explosion of so-called light beers, which now account for 25% of the market. This is further proof that Americans are watching their caloric intake. The beer experience might also show that the theory of light taste is all wet. While domestic beer sales have declined there has been a substantial increase in the sale of imported beers, which are heavier tasting than American beers. They are also more expensive, which means that price isn't as important to import beer drinkers as taste or status. The most dramatic example of the appeal of light beers can be found in Miller Brewing Company, which introduced Miller Lite in 1974 as an extension to its primary product, Miller High Life. But by 1983, Miller Lite surpassed Miller High Life in total sales; and by 1987 it was outselling High Life two-to-one. Lite still ranks second only to industry leader Budweiser in terms of total cases sold. Wine was the only alcoholic beverage to show any increase in sales in the past decade. Between 1970 and 1985, per-capita consumption of wine doubled but has remained static since then. One category of beverage that has benefited because it has a light taste, no calories and is healthful, is bottled water. Increases in sales have been averaging about 15% a year for the past decade.

As far as future sales of beer and wine are concerned, they are almost certain to drop significantly in the next decade as the Baby Busters—a smaller population group than the Baby Boomers—reach peak drinking age, which is the middle 20s. There simply will be fewer people in the age cohort that does the most drinking. The fantastic growth of light beers is not unusual when you consider what has been going on in food marketing for the past couple of decades. Supermarket shelves are carrying an ever-mushrooming array of low-calorie items, from frozen entrées and diet soft drinks all the way to such seemingly oxymoronic combinations as reduced-calorie ice cream and diet sour cream.

In 1960 the average American consumed 1.9 pounds of saccharin (not in actual pounds, but in the equivalent sweetening power to sugar). By 1986, American consumption of saccharin had grown to 5.5 pounds per capita. But that amount was dwarfed by the 13 pounds per capita of aspartame, the non-nutritive sweetener that came on the market in 1982. This means that the consumption of noncaloric sweeteners increased more than ninefold. In the same span, the amount of sugar and other caloric sweeteners increased from 116 pounds per capita to 168 pounds, up 45%. Whether American consumers have lost weight or not, their growing consumption of noncaloric sweeteners and low-calorie foods shows clearly that they are trying to keep pounds off.

Although much of the weight-loss effort was attributed to health reasons, much of it relates back to the age-old notion of people trying to stay slim and attractive. When you add these two factors together, there is no doubt that the demand for low-calorie foods will continue in the decade ahead. Some have suggested, perhaps with tongue in cheek, that all of this weight watching has increased because Americans are marrying later in life. This means that they have to stay trim longer—at least until they find someone to marry. It does seem that Americans stay in shape until they get married, then go to pot during their early family-forming years. They get serious about fitness again when they go in for the routine physical at 40 and the doctor tells them they have to lose weight, lower their blood pressure, cut back on cholesterol and so forth.

Muscling into the 1990s

We alluded earlier to another aspect of health consciousness, the fitness boom. One example is the explosion in private health clubs, which shot up from 7,500 in 1980 to nearly 21,000 in 1988. These do not include the traditional YMCAs, golf clubs, tennis clubs and other sport-specific institutions. Industry observers estimate that some 40 million Americans are members of some kind of health or fitness club.

Virtually every new business-oriented or luxury hotel is equipped with fitness facilities. Older hotels are ripping out other rooms to install various kinds of fitness equipment.

The vacation business also is seeing a major expansion in the spa business. Traditionally these were known as "fat farms," where wealthy women went to be pampered and lose a few pounds (no sexism here; merely accurate reporting). Although the new spas also offer pedicures, loofah scrubs and herbal wraps, their programs are based on more serious stuff. Sound nutrition and weight loss is an important part of most spa programs, but these establishments have also become more fitness oriented. One example is the Canyon Ranch in Tucson, Arizona, which offers such rigorous activities as hiking, mountain biking, weight training, and stress-reduction programs. Diners at Canyon Ranch also will find no salt on the tables, no wine on the menu, no soft drinks in the vending machines and no caffeine in the coffee or tea. For this they are paying $300 or more a day.

The orientation toward fitness has served to change the gender mix at the newer spas, attracting a considerable number of male customers who were not welcome at most of the traditional fat farms.

Most regular health-related exercise, however, is done independently by participants and not in the environment of a posh spa. In the past 30 years exercise has become a relatively common activity among adults. Thirty years ago, someone who jogged for health reasons was considered some kind of weirdo or fanatic; that is, jogging was for boxers in training, and bicycles were for kids, not adults. Rowing machines, exercise bikes, stair-climbing machines and weight-training machines were unheard of. Stationary bicycling has developed into a major fitness activity with the number of regular participants approaching 35 million. This obviously has also developed into a major industry for those who make stationary bikes. Walking—in various methods known as striding, power walking or race walking—has also become an exercise favorite. Because these two activities are favored by older persons, we predict strong growth in the decade to come.

A whole industry has grown out of the demand for personal fitness, and the industry will continue to grow in the 1990s, although maybe not as dramatically as in the 1980s when sales of athletic footwear more than doubled. In fact, many a Baby Boomer—indicative of the Age of Specialization—owns a closetful of activity-specific athletic shoes. One kind might be for tennis, another for jogging, yet another for walking, boating or basketball. In the old days we had one pair of sneakers that we used for everything.

Although fitness was the primary reason for the explosion in the exercise business, a couple of other reasons supported the transition. One is that exercise, which used to be grueling, was made more enjoyable. Aerobics classes—which turned boring calisthenics into a challenging dance—are one example. A social aspect also has been added to exercise, especially in the private health clubs, which have developed into places for singles (or potential singles) to meet. One might say that the health club, the jogging trail and the beach have replaced the cocktail lounge and the tavern as places where people socialize. Adding evidence to the argument is the fact that, as the number of health clubs has increased dramatically in the past decade, the number of bars and taverns has declined by about 10%.

More men than women engage in exercise regularly; women, however, are catching up. By today's standards women no longer have to be the delicate flowers expected of their gender in the early part of this century. Muscularity and fitness à la Jane Fonda, are now considered acceptable if not downright sexy.

Aside from the desire to live longer and look better, there may be another reason why exercise has become so important to large segments of the American public. Some social psychologists might say that we yearn more for physical exercise because we lead more sedentary lives. This is another aspect of our transition from a manufacturing-dominated to a service-dominated economy. Our ancestors who wielded shovels or carried bricks didn't have to find an outlet for their excess energy at the end of the workday; they came home tired. They didn't have to visit a health club or run three or four miles to work out the kinks after sitting behind a desk all day. Life for most Americans is less physically demanding than it was for their parents. We don't walk to the store anymore; we drive there in a car, even if the store is only a block or two away. And when we drive, we don't even have to shift the gears as we once did.

Even when doing something as sedentary as watching television, Americans have fallen in love with remote controls, thus avoiding the physical pain of getting off their duffs to change channels. There are skeptics who scoff at the idea of exercise as an important element in the lives of many people; the skeptics tend to be those who shun exercise themselves. The numbers over the long term prove them wrong. A Gallup Opinion Index published in 1985 showed that 46% of American adults exercised regularly, compared with only 24% in 1961.

The question for the future is whether the trend toward more healthful living will continue. Projections of demographic data indicate that it will. Nonsmokers, light drinkers and regular exercisers tend to be better educated and more affluent. This segment of the population will grow steadily over the next decade.

The over-65 group in the 1980s tended not to engage in physical exercise, but that is because they came from a background in which exercise and nutrition were not considered important. The over-65s of 2000 will be more prone to exercise, and the Baby Boomers who start hitting 65 in 2011 will reach retirement age with a lifelong habit of exercise and good nutrition.

Another relatively new element has stepped into the fitness picture: employers. An increasing number of American corporations are establishing health promotion or "wellness" programs, and many of these include exercise. Some companies have installed on-site full-service exercise centers, while others subsidize memberships in outside health clubs. The U.S. Department of Health and Human Services also estimated that half of the worksites with more than 50 employees have some kind of organized health or fitness program.

Can We Afford Health Care?

Another transition, indirectly related to exercise and nutrition, should be discussed here. It deals with the delivery of health care to the American public. We are in the midst of a revolution in health care services on virtually every level. Most evident is the growth in recent years of the health maintenance organization (HMO) and preferred provider organization (PPO) movement. Some of these new health care delivery systems are facing severe economic problems, yet there is little doubt that they came into existence because of public demand for alternative modes of service. Much of the demand is for more reasonably priced health care. Health care costs have risen far more rapidly than other consumer expenses over the past

30 years. "Cost containment" has become the byword of the health insurance industry and government regulators, but the word hasn't worked.

Unless these costs abate — and there is no evidence that they will — the demand for alternatives will continue. The demand has already caused the health care industry to become far more competitive, especially in the past decade. The traditional doctor-and-hospital combination that for years served as our health care resource is now being confronted by a slew of competitors.

Aside from the HMOs and PPOs, the other newcomers are largely specialized health care providers, many of which are frowned upon by the medical establishment. The most common of the new genre of medical providers are probably the walk-in treatment centers, where you can go for outpatient treatment when you get sick or suffer an injury. There also is a widening range of centers and clinics that specialize in fairly narrow areas of treatment. Without a referral from your personal physicians, you can get treatment for such common ailments as hemorrhoids, hernias, varicose veins or sports injuries. Somewhat related to these — as well as to the notion of looking good — are centers that deal in cosmetic surgery, liposuction and acne treatment.

Some of these new methods of distributing health care are franchised, and most use advertising to replace referrals as a means of attracting patients (or should they be called customers?).

The medical establishment once frowned upon advertising by anyone in the field, but even that old stricture is being ignored by one traditional establishment institution: hospitals. An increasing number of hospitals have hired marketing directors and mounted advertising campaigns in virtually all media, including television. They are not advertising for people to get sick and be admitted as inpatients. Instead, the typical hospital advertising message is used to promote corporate health care plans, stress-reduction programs, alcohol and drug-abuse programs and other specific services offered by hospitals. These strategies are probably necessary for the survival of hospitals as we know them. The occupancy rate at the nation's hospitals has fallen steadily over the past 20 years, even though the population has risen while the number of hospital beds has remained static. The only growth has come in outpatient care.

As part of their marketing plans hospitals have started opening branch clinics, some in such unusual though logical locations as discount stores. This is, after all, a regular congregating place for people. Even dental offices have been installed in some Montgomery Ward stores and other convenient locations.

How far can marketing techniques go in the health care business? Look no further than Chicago, where one hospital group offers money-back guarantees to patients who are not satisfied with meals, admission practices or other nonmedical services.

The health care revolution has also spread to prescription drugs, where distribution practices are changing rapidly and radically. Many physicians have started to bypass the pharmacist by selling prescription drugs directly to their patients. At least one company, Doctors' Pharmacy, of Fenton, Missouri, has entered the business of repackaging and distributing drugs directly to physicians. After one year of operation the company had developed a client base of more than two thousand physicians and has posted sales of more than two million dollars. Prescription drugs also are more readily available via mail order, which cuts down on the cost of the drugs and makes it more convenient for busy working people. This is even more attractive to older patients who might be incapacitated or on maintenance drugs.

All of these trends are on the upswing and will continue throughout the next decade. What we have witnessed in recent years is the demystification of the medical business. This corresponds with a generation of more sophisticated consumers who are taking a more active role in decision making regarding their health. They are not only more sophisticated; they also are more cynical about traditional methods of delivering health care to the populace. When physicians were relatively rare and people were ignorant about their own health, doctors were held in high esteem by virtually everyone. But the number of physicians in the country will have doubled from 140 per 100,000 population in 1950 to an estimated 280 per 100,000 in 2000. That certainly portends a surplus of doctors.

The public, however, isn't going to respond by demanding more professional medical services. They know that the cost of medical care is skyrocketing, and they also know that insurance companies are scrutinizing claims more carefully. Patients can't get surgery without second or even third opinions, and they can't stay in hospitals indefinitely. In addition, employers are limiting their contributions to health insurance, throwing much of the burden back onto the individual. Because of this we can expect a rapid expansion in home health care. This is the movement toward more self-diagnosis and self-treatment, another way for Americans to combat the precipitous rise in health care costs.

By the end of the 1990s, a blood pressure–measuring device will be as common in the average home as a fever thermometer. We will conduct our own blood tests for cholesterol and urine tests for sugar levels. There are already products on the market consumers can use to test themselves for pregnancy and colon cancer. All of these techniques will increase throughout the 1990s as Americans learn that you don't have to be a brain surgeon to do a little doctoring.

What is important to remember as we look into the future is that the number of older persons will rise sharply after the turn of the century. That will place far more importance on health care. One thing that appears to be changing is people's attitude comparing the quality of life with the prolongation of life. As greater numbers of Americans live well into their 80s and 90s, there are indications that the "right to die" will become a more popularly held tenet. We will be less likely to take extraordinary measures to prolong the life of an elderly person if it means that the patient will have to live on a life-support system. And the question that will keep coming back as a refrain throughout the 1990s will be: Who will pay for it?

Trends

- Americans know more about health and fitness and are responding by taking better care of themselves.
- Nutritional habits of consumers have improved dramatically in the past decade and will continue to do so over the next decade.
- The fitness boom will roll on, although Americans might shift their tastes among the different forms of exercise alternatives.
- Life-threatening habits such as smoking and drinking are on a long-term slide.
- Consumer demands have created a revolution in health care delivery systems and the demystification of medical care.

Strategies

- Food marketers will have to upgrade products nutritionally as consumers become more aware of ingredients, calories, fat content and such.
- Blending good nutrition with good taste will result in a successful recipe for food manufacturing firms.
- Employers should consider offering on-site exercise facilities or subsidized health club memberships as a fringe benefit.
- Expansion of the fitness industry will create jobs for personal trainers, sports instructors, exercise physiologists, massage therapists and the like.
- The market will grow for adult nonalcoholic and low-alcoholic drinks that can substitute for liquor on social occasions.
- Any health care provider that can lower the cost of services to employers and consumers in the next decade will be rewarded handsomely.

CHAPTER 13

The Search for Experience

Many American families — especially those usually described as upwardly mobile — are faced with a challenge that no other society in history has ever faced. They are drowning in a sea of material possessions. In recent years, domestic and foreign manufacturers have produced a steady stream of new products — largely technological — that have become virtual necessities for American families. How did I *ever* get along without the microwave oven? is what single people and working parents say about the little kitchen wonder. Yet *everyone* got along without the microwave until only a few years ago, when it was marketed at an affordable price. With a steady increase in its everyday use the microwave has developed into a necessary, or at least an extremely convenient, item for millions of American families. But it is only one of many other gadgets that we consider as being necessary, even though previous generations led useful lives without them.

Few of us, of course, could exist without our telephones, television sets, radios or electric shavers. Others would have a terrible time getting through the day without electric toothbrushes, cellular car phones or compact disc players. Most middle-class American families live in the midst of a lot of stuff, more stuff than anybody else in the world. Consider the ratio of various products to the number of households in the United States, and you can see that we are awash with possessions. There are 91.5 million households in this

country. They range from the stereotypical mom-pop-and-kids households on which most of the old television sitcoms were based, to the
rapidly growing single-person, single-parent or nonfamily households
on which many of *today's* television sitcoms are based. (Television
does mirror reality to some extent.) The average American household has 1.9 television sets, 5.6 radios, 1.6 cars and 1.7 telephones.
Because there are only about 2.6 persons per household, you can
see where our possessions are catching up on our people. While the
ratios aren't so large, 70% of our households have microwave ovens,
and about 65% have videocassette recorders. Only 16% of our households have personal computers, but this percentage is expected to
double by 1993. Of the household computers, 30% are equipped with
telephone modems.

In the years to come we will see a comparable proliferation of
cellular telephones, facsimile machines, copiers, exercise bikes, rowing machines and other items whose sales are just starting to hit stride.
Perhaps they will not achieve the penetration of color television sets,
which are in 95% of households, but they will reach a point of satu-
ration eventually.

Is this too much stuff? Apparently so. It isn't very likely that a
family with a microwave oven will buy a second one, except perhaps to replace the original when it breaks down. If only 30% of
homes do not have microwave ovens, then the potential for future
growth isn't as great as it was when no one had them.

Americans also sense that they have too many possessions, if only
because their houses and garages have run out of space. Affluent families are discarding unused or outdated possessions at such a rapid
rate that it has spawned a whole new industry: the resale business.
Every corner of the country is treated to a constant array of garage
sales, yard sales, flea markets, rummage sales, vintage clothing shops,
antique (or "junque") shops and other kinds of used merchandise sales.
These secondhand operations are taking place in big cities, suburbs,
small towns and rural areas. They are run by the rich and the poor,
although perhaps for different reasons. The poor are trying to eke
a few extra dollars out of items they can't use anymore or that they
have gleaned from the throwaways of others; the rich are trying to
clear out some space in their garages or basements to make room
for a new inventory of material possessions. One person's castoffs

194

can be another's treasure. This is merely anecdotal evidence of over-possession. Statistics, of course, are more difficult to come by. But professors at many universities are starting to preach about the prospect of marketing in an era of surplus. Basically they say that we have too much of everything.

There are too many products on the market, too many brands, too many new products introduced every year, too many extensions, too many flavors, too many sizes, too many variations, too many competitors. All of these items are growing at a rapid pace while population is leveling off. Marketers know that this is the Age of Segmentation, so they are customizing products for various slivers of the market. The basic problem is that, as products get more targeted to specific audiences, unit sales decline. With lower volume, products are less profitable for the manufacturer.

And yet the proliferation continues. Look at Coca-Cola, as an example. For decades there was only one Coke, and it was the most successful soft drink in the world. Then Coca-Cola introduced Tab as a low-calorie flanker product. Today we have New Coke, Classic Coke, Diet Coke, Caffeine-Free Diet Coke, Cherry Coke, Diet Cherry Coke *and* Tab. We may have overlooked a few others.

There was a time when the only over-the-counter painkiller available was aspirin. Now the consumer has to choose from a selection that includes not only aspirin but buffered aspirin, acetaminophen or ibuprofen. There also are several brands of each, including the drugstore's house brand, plus regular strength and extra strength, and varieties of tablets, capsules, caplets, coated tablets, easy-opening or childproof lids, etc. Even if we didn't have a headache going into the drugstore, trying to find the right item would give us one.

The Supermarket Squeeze

This explosion of consumer products in recent years has changed the role of at least one major retail entity, the supermarket. The supermarket traditionally served as a conveyor belt, moving product from manufacturer to consumer. The manufacturers were the ones with the clout. Companies like Procter & Gamble would go to retailers with a new product and tell them how many millions of dollars they were going to spend on advertising. The advertising would create consumer demand, forcing the supermarket to stock the item. Supermarkets would vie with each other to be the first to put a new product on their shelves. At the same time many retailers felt manufacturers were cramming new products down their throats, using their advertising muscle to grab more shelf space.

Those were the old days. Throughout the 1980s supermarkets started turning the tables. Now it was the retailer who had the clout—thanks to the economic principle of supply and demand. There are far too many products available for any supermarket to stock. In addition, the number of food stores in the country isn't much higher in 1990 than it was 25 years earlier—about 300,000 units. They are larger, it is true, but they also carry far more nonfood items. As a result, the demand for store shelf space far outpaces the supply. So instead of being a conveyor belt the supermarket has turned into a filter.

Retailers are looking carefully at every new product offered them, as well as old ones they have been carrying for years. If the old product isn't moving, or if the new one doesn't look like it has potential, you won't find them on the shelves. Using far more sophisticated techniques than ever before, large supermarket chains can tell whether new products are really new or are simply clones of other products already on the shelves. If the retailer determines that the new product won't generate new sales but simply cannibalize another brand already on the shelves, the new entry has a poor chance of getting exposure. No shelf space, no sales. Rather than flaunt their marketing plans, manufacturers find that they have to pay various fees—called slotting charges—for shelf space and in-store promotions, as well as for being included in the supermarket's advertising. This is going to create some interesting maneuvers in the 1990s.

Supermarket shelf space is tightening so much that many experts believe it will slow the flow of new products onto the market—quite a feat considering that there are nearly three thousand new food products introduced every year. And this does not include new flavors, sizes, or other varieties of products already on the market.

A reduction in new products may well turn out to be a benefit for the consumer. With a more demanding marketplace, new products will have to show a demonstrable improvement over whatever is currently on the market. This means less confusion and fewer parity clones for shoppers to mull over.

Perhaps the most important marketing tool of the next decade will be packaging as manufacturers invest heavily to devise packaging that will be attractive to the busy shopper hustling through supermarket aisles. The shopping public will include fewer full-time housewives and far more working mothers. Techniques such as using shrink-wrap to attach a free premium item to a product will be commonplace. A set of plastic bottle stoppers might be attached to a six-pack of soft drinks. Or a free candy bar will be inserted in a box of cereal. The idea is to stimulate impulse buying; two-thirds of the shoppers don't know what they are going to buy before they enter the store.

Even more universal will be the downsizing of food packaging. Manufacturers previously put products like cereal in as large a box as possible to make consumers believe they were getting more for their money. With more informed consumers, plus the squeeze on shelf space, look for smaller packages. Many companies will be making their packages narrower and taller so they will take up less shelf space and be more attractive to supermarketers who are trying to display as many items as possible. Products in cylindrical containers will be reintroduced in rectangular containers to save space. There is already a movement to package coffee in space-saving vacuum-process bags rather than in the traditional cans. The challenge for manufacturers will be to make their products small enough to flow through the supermarket filter. A student of the theory of supply and demand might speculate that the demand for shelf space will eventually lead supermarkets to create more space. Don't count on it. The reason: Demand is coming from the wrong direction. If consumers were demanding more products, supermarkets would respond. The only demand for more products is coming from manufacturers. Customers aren't clamoring for more brands of toilet paper or instant coffee; they already have more than they need.

Our example has concentrated on grocery products and supermarkets, but the same overabundance of products exists in virtually every area of retailing. From athletic shoes to computer software, the selection of available goods has outgrown the retailers' capacity to carry them. That certainly is the case with computer software, of which there are more than ten thousand different items on the market, far more than even the largest retailer can carry.

197

The irony here is that the number of retail establishments in the country has barely grown in the past ten years. As we pointed out earlier, the number of food retailers has remained constant – in fact, has even declined slightly – since the mid-1960s. In that same span, we have decidedly fewer automobile dealers, service stations, furniture stores, liquor stores, hardware stores and household appliance stores. This particular trend, however, may not continue through the 1990s. We are witnessing a boom in small specialty stores, which may well increase the number of retail outlets in several of the categories listed above.

The important point to remember in all of this is that the number of retail outlets is not a function of how many products are being put in the marketplace, but how much consumer demand there is. With our population growth coming to a halt and with a surplus of possessions in most households, we will not see the increases in demand that American business has become accustomed to in the past 50 years.

From Not Enough to Too Much in 50 Years

The best way to appreciate the surplus economy on which the United States is bobbing is through the perspective of history. Sixty years ago this country was riding one of the great economic booms of all time, the Roaring Twenties. Then one day – October 29, 1929, the day the stock market crashed – we ran head-first into the Great Depression. That was the beginning of a troubled and traumatic era.

The depression segued into the international tragedy of World War II. Americans who lived through those two long, crippling episodes came away with an austere mentality that Baby Boomers and their children would find difficult to understand. By 1945, the end of World War II, Americans had suffered through 15 consecutive years of deprivation.

During that torturous decade of the 1930s our marriage rate tumbled. There were only 981,000 marriages in 1932, the lowest since the early years of the century. Population in the 1930s registered the slowest decade of growth since the first census was taken in 1790. Fewer marriages meant fewer children.

Home prices spiraled lower as demand dried up. New homes were not being built, and cars were not being sold. Housing starts slid from 937,000 in 1925 to 220,000 in 1935. It was no wonder. The unemployment rate never moved below 14% during the whole decade and was higher than 20% for four straight years, 1932–35.

It was World War II that finally pulled the United States out of the depths of the depression. But even though Americans were going back to work, they still couldn't buy the products they wanted. They may have had the money for a new car, but cars weren't being built during the war years. Most of America's consumer goods factories were converted to producing goods for the war effort. Many other items, from sugar to shoes, were rationed.

By the time the war ended, Americans were ready to make up for a decade and a half of lost time. There was a tremendous pent-up demand to be satisfied, and we satisfied it with a vengeance. This country exhibited a ferocious postwar appetite for everything that had been denied it since 1929. It started with an explosion in the marriage rate. America's fighting men – who totaled 16 million during the war – came back home to start new lives. There were nearly 2.3 million marriages in the United States in 1946, a 42% jump over the previous year. This was followed approximately nine months later with the beginning of what has since become known as the Baby Boom. At the same time, Americans started to fulfill their urge to acquire previously unattainable possessions. These new families wanted homes, but there weren't enough to go around in the late 1940s. That housing shortage led to a boom in residential construction. From a low of 141,900 housing starts in 1944, the construction industry boomed to 931,600 units in 1948.

Americans also wanted wheels. Car demand was so ferocious that buyers were bribing dealers for a postwar model; they actually paid more than list price. This is a far cry from the current car market, where nobody pays full sticker price. Today, car buyers negotiate discounts from dealers, they get rebates from the manufacturers, and they even get their car loans at artificially low rates.

It was during these postwar years that the United States earned its reputation as the land of conspicuous consumption. We were snapping up everything in sight to make up for the lean years, embarking on a shopping spree that fueled extraordinary economic growth for the next 20 years. But it was a spree that couldn't go on forever. There were several reasons for this, the most obvious of which is that our population was climbing rapidly in the 1950s and 1960s, faster than it had ever grown in history. Our population grew by 19% in the 1950s and 14% in the 1960s.

But as the Baby Boom started to peter out we added only 10% to our population in the 1970s and 9% in the 1980s. Our growth rate for the 1990s is estimated at 7%. American corporations recognized the population bubble in the two postwar decades and responded by pumping a stream of products into the marketplace. But many of the same corporations apparently failed to acknowledge the slower growth of the past few years. That factor, combined with the increasing invasion of imports from abroad, created an overcapacity of manufacturing in many industries. We are still geared up to turn out products for a rapidly expanding society with a 15-year backlog of pent-up demand. The American consumer, however, hasn't been deprived of any physical goods in the past 40 years. Even if we couldn't afford something, we borrowed to buy it; or we put it on our credit cards. As as result, there is no pent-up demand for anything.

We have reached the point where virtually every family has a house or apartment in which to live. There also is a car for every member of the family who can drive, a telephone for everyone who can speak, a radio for everyone who can hear, a television set for every room, enough clothing in the average family to dress an army platoon, and so much food that our prime concern in life is eating less. And when you reach that point, what happens?

The Coming Experience Boom

One answer might be found in the theories of the late psychologist-philosopher Abraham Maslow. He held that man seeks at first to satisfy the basic necessities of life, normally considered to be physical needs. And when these lower-level needs are met man then seeks to satisfy higher-level needs. There is growing evidence that what Americans want more than anything else right now are not more physical goods but experiences, a phenomenon that led to the creation of what some socioeconomists call the "experience industry." Many of these experiences come in the form of leisure activities or vacations.

Perhaps the most obvious form of experience consumption is travel. Travel by Americans has soared in the past 20 years. Domestic airlines flew 455 million passengers in 1988, up 197% over the 153 million carried in 1970. In 1970 less than half the American population had ever flown on an airplane. By 1987, 73% had flown, a result of the desire for personal experiences coupled with the airlines' introduction of promotional fares.

Despite the declining value of the dollar, foreign travel continues to increase because we want to experience life in other countries. International travel grew from 16 million passengers in 1970 to 25 million in 1985. We want to see things for ourselves. A good many second- and third-generation Americans are traveling back to the lands of their ancestors to seek out family roots. Even the way we travel has changed to create richer experiences. We don't merely visit France and look at the Arc de Triomphe; instead, we might take a barge trip down the Seine or a gastronomic tour through the wine country. We go on an African safari to see the endangered animals with our own eyes; we journey to Nepal to trek in the Himalayas; we travel to Mexico to crawl over Mayan ruins; or we fly to the Bahamas to snorkel in an underwater world.

Even domestic vacations indicate that experience seeking is the new goal. Today's vacation might well include such novel experiences as hot-air ballooning, white-water rafting, whale watching, mountain hiking, cross-country biking, mule trips in the Grand Canyon or ocean cruising. And a burgeoning number of travelers will capture those experiences with a videotape camera, another important element in the growing experience industry. The ultimate status symbol for many Americans has become the living out of one's fantasies. Fantasizing is nothing new. As children we played the experience game, pretending to be cowboys, soldiers or nurses. Adults also fantasize, but perhaps about more sophisticated subjects, such as lifestyles and sex. Speaking of which, we should point out that those naughty X-rated telephone services are yet another example of a growing segment of the experience industry. Come to think of it, maybe telephone sex falls somewhere between fantasy and experience.

The experience industry has been around for many years, as evidenced by the success of enterprises such as Disneyland, Sea World and Busch Gardens, all of which manufacture various environmental and theme experiences for tourists. But the demand for more spectacular and realistic experiences apparently is still growing, prompting the marketing people to fill that demand. In 1989 Universal Studios in Hollywood started what might be the ultimate in tourism experience: a simulated earthquake registering 8.3 on the Richter scale, complete with collapsing walls, broken water mains, careening trucks and erupting streets. Tourists, safe from harm of course, ride through the quake in a simulated subway car. In our quest for experiences we have even transformed something as disastrous as an earthquake into a form of entertainment.

Although amusement parks date back more than 100 years, business has boomed in the past few years. In 1988, the nation's amusement and theme parks hosted record numbers of more than 250 million visitors a year. That averages out to one visit for every man, woman and child in the United States. The important point is that the variety of experience-oriented opportunities is growing as our appetite for them increases. The continued flourishing of these businesses should demonstrate to us that this is where the leisure industry is headed.

The same situation exists regarding rock concerts, where teens and young adults pay far more than list price for a ticket into a crammed auditorium; sometimes they don't even have an unobstructed view of the stage. The ability to display a tour T-shirt sold only at rock concerts is a mark of distinction for young people, even though the shirts may run $20 or more apiece. The shirt signifies that the wearer personally experienced a concert by U2, the Grateful Dead or some other popular group.

Our appetite for experiences also has had a significant impact on sports. As television audiences for most sports have plateaued or declined, attendance at sporting events has grown steadily over the years. We want to see, hear and feel the experience of a major league baseball game or a professional basketball game. This has led to constant pressure in many sports to expand leagues to additional cities. It also has led to astronomical scalper prices for tickets to special events such as the Super Bowl and the World Series. In the past 20 years, attendance at professional football games has increased by 154%, baseball by 89%, and professional basketball by 214%. These increases are all far more than the population growth for the same period of time.

Doing Is Better Than Watching

The growth in sports participation by Americans is even more dramatic than the increase in spectatorship. From laid-back activities such as fishing to high-energy pursuits such as skiing, we are participating in more leisure activities. Also at play here, of course, is the increased desire by Americans to lead healthier lives and feel fit, a concept treated in an earlier chapter.

Nothing demonstrates our yearning for entertaining experiences as much as the "fantasy baseball camps" that have proliferated in recent years. These allow men at the threshold of middle age or beyond to spend a week at a spring training camp in Arizona or Florida. For a hefty price attendees don their own official team uniforms and work out every day with retired baseball stars. At the end of a day on the diamond they can go out drinking and trading war stories with their heroes. What more satisfying experience can there be for the average American male, who still is a boy at heart?

Besides sports, Americans also are becoming more involved in other avocational activities such as amateur photography — still and videotape — painting, singing, music, dancing or adult education classes. Something as mundane as cooking has turned into an experiential art form in recent years. The typical working couple doesn't have enough time during the week to cook full meals, so they eat out more often or bring home prepared foods. On weekends, however, legions of them engage in the experience of gourmet cooking. They buy exotic types of lettuce, shop for rare wines, grind their own blends of coffee beans or concoct their own special béarnaise sauce. They have elevated cooking from a daily chore to an occasional hobby.

Even business is responding to this experience orientation. The concept was adopted by the marketing wizards long ago, as witnessed by the many major advertising campaigns based on pointing out the pleasant experience of buying a particular product or service. "Put yourself behind the wheel of this car," the hucksters say. "Feel the power of the fuel-injected engine. Experience the smooth acceleration. Sit back in the comfort of ergonomically engineered bucket seats." These are powerful suggestions to make to a prospective buyer. But advertisers also know that an even more powerful motivator is an aversion to a negative experience. What can be worse, for example, than the embarrassment of ring around the collar?

What has happened over the years is that the marketers no longer say: "Buy this product because it is good." Instead they say: "You can have a wonderful experience if you buy this product." And of course, in the tradition of American advertising there are no limits to what they can promise. Take a bite of Imperial margarine, for instance, and you will feel like a member of the royal family.

The experience factor has also filtered into other aspects of business, including some of the newer management techniques being employed. Quality circles, borrowed from the Japanese, allow line workers to participate in corporate decision making formerly reserved for managers. Some companies require managers to spend time on assembly lines or on sales calls so they can learn different facets of the business. Others use various training techniques, such as role playing, to help create better rapport between management and employees.

As society becomes increasingly complex, Americans have turned more to psychoanalysis, which should be considered another aspect of the experience industry. Applying Maslow's theory, we might say that we have taken care of our physical needs and now have graduated to a higher level by taking care of our psychological needs. That argument may or may not be true, but more convincing might be society's growing interest and involvement in such experiential activities as the *est* movement, group therapy, evangelical religions and yoga.

Here's to the Good Old Days

The nostalgia trend is another form of experience marketing. We see it evidenced in the growing number of radio stations playing music that was popular in previous decades. There also has been a boomlet—a fad not yet documented as a trend—in 1950s-era restaurants, such as the Ed Debevics or Johnny Rockets eateries, springing up in a few cities. In the same genre are nightclubs oriented toward the 1950s.

No car is hotter this year than the 1957 Chevy. The whole front end of that classic car protrudes like a canopy from the facade of a building on Chicago's trendy Lincoln Avenue. In the building is a nightclub called Jukebox Saturday Night, which caters to young adults, and on most nights, there is no one inside who actually remembers the 1950s.

This shows the dual-market nature of nostalgia. The older folks like to be reminded about those happier and simpler years. The younger ones want to get a feeling of what it was like. You should notice, though, that there was never such a nostalgia boom for the 1930s and 1940s. Those were decades we would just as soon forget.

The demand for experiences demonstrates a higher plane of human demand, but that doesn't mean *all* of the pursuits are good. After all, the expanded use of illegal drugs in recent years is also a manifestation of the demand for new experiences. We should recognize that there are different motives for drug use. A poor, unemployed ghetto dweller with a criminal record and little or no chance of ever getting a decent job will steal for drugs as an escape from real life. On the other hand, we have the athlete who is making $1,500,000 a year in salary and endorsements and is considered a hero by millions of fans. He drives a $60,000 Porsche, wears a $20,000 fur coat and lives in a $1,000,000 mansion. He also takes drugs, even though ostensibly he has nothing to escape from. But he is looking for something more than the pleasure that all of his physical goods can give him. The thief and the sports star are both seeking a different experience.

What all of this means for the year 2000 and beyond is that our goals as individuals are changing. There was a time in our society when owning a car was a status symbol; then owning a certain *brand* of car was a status symbol. But now, auto ownership doesn't impart very much distinction. Experiences, on the other hand, still denote status. A lecturer might be introduced to his audience as a world traveler or Vietnam veteran. But who would ever introduce *anyone* as a Ford owner? Even a Mercedes-Benz owner?

Trends indicate that the experiential applications will become more important in the coming decade. Vacation tour operators should go beyond their humdrum tour-bus offerings and devise a wider array of hands-on experiences for tourists. They also must provide the tourist with some external evidence of having gone through the experience, something akin to the T-shirts kids buy at rock concerts. The use of experience techniques can also provide academicians with more powerful tools to teach young people. These new techniques should come out of the institutions that teach teachers, but there is little evidence that this is happening. Walk into a college or high school classroom today and you will witness education as it was when you went to school—an instructor lecturing to students. It doesn't matter how old you are; little has changed. There are indications that the business sector will become more active in public education and may transfer some of its training techniques to the schools.

Attendance at sporting events in the 1990s is expected to grow substantially as the number of middle-age Americans increases. Using the same trend data we might expect a drop in attendance when the Baby Boomers start hitting retirement age in the first decade of the twenty-first century. Similarly we expect that rock-concert attendance and other youth-related events will lag in the next decade because there will be fewer young adults in our population mix.

We also predict the expansion of professional football, baseball and basketball to many new and smaller markets by 2000. In the coming years we will see the establishment of sports management as a new and growing field. Not only will sports managers run professional teams but also the amateur leagues and conferences formed to satisfy the demand for participation sports. As the number of older persons grows we also can expect to see more professional and amateur participation by seniors in organized sports. (Remember, in some sports being over 35 qualifies a player as a senior.) So far, the senior golfing tour has been the most successful on the professional level. But old-timer baseball games are attracting larger audiences, and senior tennis players are becoming more active in tournaments and exhibition matches.

Perhaps the greatest growth in the future, though, will come in providing all kinds of experience-oriented programs for senior citizens, from sports to travel to self-enrichment activities. More than anyone else, the older generation has had its fill of physical goods. Thousands of them sell their large homes and move into smaller apartments. They have less room and less need for the material trappings of life. And like everyone else, they won't be content to watch the world go by on television; they'll want to experience some of it.

Trends

- The big post–World War II boom is over. Most Americans have more possessions than they need, moderating any great future increase in demand for products.

- Too many new products are entering the pipeline, putting pressure on retailers who don't have the space to display them.

- Because of the product squeeze, retailers are gaining importance in the marketing chain.

- The number of retailers has plateaued, or even declined, giving them even more clout in moving products to consumers.

- The status symbols of the next decade will not be luxury products but exotic and unusual experiences.

Strategies

- All consumer products businesses should consider establishing strategies for marketing in the Age of Surplus.

- Manufacturers will have to be more selective in launching new products. Items should be targeted more specifically to consumer demands.

- The role of packaging will become more critical. Manufacturers should downsize packages to assure display space. Package design will be more critical to sales.

- Opportunities will arise for specialized retail stores that carry complete lines of product categories.

- The "experience industry" will grow in the 1990s. Experiences, rather than material goods, will make better employee awards and fund-raising incentives.

CHAPTER 14

America: Melting Pot or Tossed Salad?

As children, many of us were taken up with the notion of the United States as a melting-pot society. This was the world's dream country because we were made up of people from virtually every other nation. No other country has seen the same waves of immigrants wash across their shores as we have in the United States. The British were the first to come in great numbers; then the Germans, Africans, Irish, Scandinavians, Italians, Polish, Mexicans and Vietnamese. They came in one wave after another, in greater numbers than any other receiving country has ever seen. There was—and is—a special attraction that the United States holds for immigrants. For centuries this country has been a safe haven for refugees from war, poverty and persecution. More than that, we also are seen as the "land of opportunity," a place where a poor, uneducated person can learn to put automobiles together, make $35,000 a year, buy a house and take the kids to visit Disney World. It hasn't worked out that way for all immigrants, but it certainly did for most of them and their children.

Out of this diversity of nationalities has developed a truly unique nation. Most other countries of the world are marked by homogeneity; that is, they are the same color, practice the same religion, speak the same language, are descended from the same tribes, uphold the same values, celebrate the same customs. Walk down a street in Midtown Manhattan and you can see that people aren't quite so homogeneous in the United States. You will hear a cacophony of languages, see the full spectrum of skin color and review a wide variety of dress and mannerisms. You might also say that Manhattan isn't representative of the United States, and you would be correct. So change your venue. Instead, browse through the K mart in Des Plaines, Illinois, a suburb of Chicago, and you will witness the same potpourri of shoppers. This eclectic collection of individuals is truly what the United States is all about.

Somewhere along the line we believed, in our childlike idealism, the melting pot of this country would blend us all into one people. From the diversity of backgrounds would emerge the "American race," made up of the best characteristics of each of our nationalities. So far this ideal remains unfulfilled. Maybe what we didn't realize as children is exactly how long this amalgamation would take. We were thinking decades, but we should have been looking at centuries.

What we also didn't consider was how our cultural biases would affect the way each race and national group felt about the others. We didn't realize, for example, that each new wave of immigrants would get a cold and often hostile reception from the preceding wave. We also underestimated the difficulty blacks would have in assimilating into the mainstream of white American culture or the resistance they would experience from segments of the white populace. If this is a melting pot, then someone had better turn up the fire. This cultural casserole isn't cooking as fast as we thought it would.

Pass the Salad Dressing

As you may have deduced by now, we made a childish mistake in our nationalistic fantasy. We chose the wrong analogy. As long as we have an ongoing infusion of immigrants from different countries, we will never be able to blend into one harmonious and homogeneous society. Despite this reality there is a multitude of evidence to show that all of these Americans from different backgrounds are indeed slowly growing more alike. This is happening not so much from something internal but because of outside influences from government, business and communications.

Instead of the melting pot, look at U.S. society as a salad. Each ingredient in the salad is a different race or national group. What is binding us together are the common outside influences; they make up the salad dressing. They make us taste pretty much the same, although underneath all that salad dressing some of us are endive while others are arugula. What has happened over the years is that the salad dressing has become stronger. And the longer we stay in the salad bowl, the more we start taking on the taste of the dressing.

Government is important in this gastronomic mix because its policies have fostered the notion of equality—in theory if not in practice. Not only are we referring to federal government but also to state and local governments. One element that is drawing us closer together is a fairly similar network of public education systems. There are obvious differences in quality from one part of the country to another, or even from one suburb to another. No one can deny the wide gulf that exists between a classroom in Beverly Hills and one in Watts. Nonetheless, some minimal standards have been established. This standardization has grown with the increased interest in such universal measurements as national reading scores; we are all judged against each other. Similarly, parents of high school children from diverse parts of the country can find a common topic of conversation in the Scholastic Aptitude Test or American College Testing scores of their offspring.

Despite regional variations, elementary and secondary curricula are not all that different from one school district to the next. The same textbooks are used in schools across the country, dependent largely on how effective the publisher's field salesperson is. Teachers can graduate from the University of Iowa and take a job anywhere from Orlando, Florida to Seattle, Washington. The result is that standardized education helps to make us more alike. And although we specifically mentioned public education, private education is also subject to most of the same standards and measurements. The biggest difference is probably not in the education but in the orientation of the families that send their children to private and parochial schools.

Mandates for Equality

Similarity in education is only one factor that is making us more alike. Government mandates in numerous other areas are having the same effect. Social Security, for example, is an umbrella that covers millions of Americans, no matter what their race, where they live or how wealthy they are. The federal government sends out more than 38 million Social Security checks every month to nearly 30% of households in the nation.

Equal Employment Opportunity laws also provide a common ground for Americans by helping create a level playing field for all workers. They may not work as well in practice as in theory, but they have established national standards for employers dealing with workers.

Various other standards, ranging from food and drug requirements to airline safety measures, all contribute to a common background for most Americans. Even taxes bring us together in their own diabolical way. No matter where they live, the color of their skin or size of their paycheck, Americans universally complain about how much they pay in income taxes.

American business is also playing a significant role in providing us with similar frames of reference. The grand champion of all social levelers would have to be McDonald's and all the other national franchised fast-food operations. Albeit some minor regional differences in menu and prices, a Big Mac is a Big Mac; and it doesn't matter whether the customer is a preppie from Winnetka or a juvenile delinquent from the South Bronx. The experience is pretty much the same. This isn't an isolated example, either. One of the major business trends of the past 20 years has been the franchising of virtually every kind of service. No matter what far-flung corner of the country you might explore, you will be confronted with a variety of familiar trademarks and names, from Ace Hardware to Ziebart rustproofing.

The establishment of national brands in all areas of consumer goods also gives a common frame of reference to the diverse patchwork that makes up the quilt of American society. In their ghettos, first-generation immigrants tend to shop at food stores and other retailers where their language is spoken. And they look for brands imported from their countries of origin.

The true rite of passage into the American culture comes when an immigrant from Mexico gives in to the lure of advertising and buys his first bag of Doritos. Or an Italian-American decides that

Ragú spaghetti sauce will fill the bill when there isn't enough time to make the real thing (or thinks it is better than Mama's sauce). This is a gradual process of assimilation that may take generations to accomplish. When it happens, it signifies that a newcomer is taking another step toward blending in with the American culture. Some ethnic groups hang onto their traditional customs longer than others, and it takes them longer to blend in; but they all blend in eventually.

Even though we are concentrating on the American consumer here, we should also point out that international brands also serve as common denominators between people in different countries. Although it is occurring at a much slower pace, consumers in industrialized countries are becoming more alike, just as different ethnic groups in the United States are doing.

Increased travel has also helped pull the United States closer together in that we can see how other people live and adopt what we like. This doesn't mean that our whole country is out buzzing around. There is still a considerable amount of domestic isolationism, ranging from the inner-city youth who has never stepped outside his neighborhood to the suburban teenager who has never ventured to the big city's downtown center.

The last, and maybe most pervasive, ingredient in the salad dressing that flavors all of us is the media. You can forget the print media. As we pointed out earlier, mass-circulation magazines are giving way to segmented publications. In today's publishing business, finding the characteristics that differentiate us is more important than identifying the threads that draw us together.

The most important unifying influence, of course, is television. This medium is so influential because it cuts across all demographic and psychographic groups. Even people who say they don't watch television do watch it occasionally. Whether through news, documentaries, dramas or commercials, television viewers can see the way other people live—or at least how the medium interprets the way they live. Television is a tremendous unifying force, for several reasons. When historic events are being broadcast—presidential inaugurations, Oscar presentations or the Super Bowl—all of us gather together as a national family to watch them. For the past couple of decades television has produced most of our heros. It has been instrumental in establishing fads and fashions. Along with radio, television also helps immigrants learn English (oddly enough, more efficiently than they learn it in school). The broadcast media also are gradually softening the regional accents in our country; that is, we sound more alike because of broadcasting. People can actually come out of Brooklyn today without the nasal twang or out of Dallas without the drawl.

Television serves as a great medium for teenagers because its immediacy keeps them up with the current fashions, the right slang, the latest fads and the newest reincarnation of blue jeans. Of all age groups, teenagers have more in common with each other than any other cohort. Adolescence is an effective homogenizing agent. It has been said, not totally in jest, that a teenager has more in common with a teenager from any other country in the world than with his or her own parents.

This description of television as a great unifier does not conflict with our earlier contention that the medium is being eroded by various forms of segmented communications. Television will be with us for decades and will continue to have an effect on our lives. But the networks won't be as powerful as they have been in previous years. Television also will adapt itself to the new environment because it must do so in order to survive. The lines between television and cable also will be blurred in the years to come. In fact, this is bound to have an impact on whether we continue to coalesce as a society. Through cable, television has already become more segmented. Cable will not grow into a major force, however, until it becomes available to everyone, as network television has been. To date, cable reaches only 54% of the households in the country. By 2000, cable penetration should be approaching 75%. As cable grows, the nature of so-called network programming will change. Instead of nationally broadcast programs for the whole family, cable will provide national "narrowcasting" to specific demographic and psychographic subgroups, such as teenagers, blue-collar workers, young professional women, retired persons and the like. As a result, members of these affinity groups will find a common ground just as the fight for equal rights for women has created a "sisterhood" of sorts. In the decade ahead, retired people, as another example, will draw more closely together regardless of race or level of affluence. As far as the twenty-first century is concerned, we will take another step toward developing an American culture, but it won't be a great leap toward homogenization.

213

Only one point remains open for discussion: Do we *want* to develop into a single American culture? In our childlike fantasies about a single society, we never asked ourselves that question. And the answer may be no. Many of the immigrants who came to this country in the early part of the twentieth century urged their children to "become Americans." They wanted them to speak English, get a good job and slip into the relatively affluent American lifestyle. It certainly was a better life than they had left in the "old country."

For all of the reasons discussed earlier in this chapter, as well as the unifying influence of World War II, Americans have grown more alike. Now that they have, it seems they are looking for various features that make them distinctive. Nobody wants to be the "average American." One thing that is happening is that many of us have decided to explore our roots, as Alex Haley did a few years back with the acclaimed television series, "Roots." Americans are sifting through family memorabilia to find recipes for favorite dishes or searching for old family photographs. In a few years, they will be looking for old family videos.

New Politics: The Liberative

Many commentators in the past decade have concluded that Americans are more conservative than they were 20 to 30 years ago. That misreading of the American psyche is simply the commentators' desire to explain away with one word some profound changes. It makes it easier to write a headline, but it isn't necessarily the case.

Perhaps the eight-year term of Ronald Reagan, followed by the election of George Bush, gave these commentators the notion that we had become more conservative. Whatever the reason, there is no evidence to back up their contention. In fact, if we were to throw around the notions of conservative and liberal as loosely as the commentators do, we probably could come up with a scenario that proves the opposite conclusion, that the nation has become more liberal. What has happened is that Americans do not fit tidily into the labels anymore. The same people who elected Republican presidents for the past three elections have elected enough Democratic congressmen to maintain that party's majority in the House of Representatives.

Americans aren't buying the whole package anymore; they are picking and choosing what they want.

The emerging generation of Baby Boomers has members on both the right and left wings of politics, but in the decade ahead we see most of them easing into a combination of conservative and liberal. We call them "liberatives." Maybe we should call them "conservervals." This generation, which makes up about one-third of our population, may be more capitalist-minded than the preceding generation, but they are also more socially liberal. Most of them are *pro* choice in the abortion controversy; they respect women as equals in the job market; they are more accepting of alternative lifestyles and living arrangements; they aren't as blindly biased against minorities.

At the same time, this generation has embraced some views that are generally considered conservative. They appear to be more interested in their own careers than in public service; they are skeptical of government welfare programs; they aren't as antiestablishment as the generation of the 1960s; they like the status quo; and they are more family-oriented. As always, there are plenty of exceptions to this generalized view of Baby Boomers. There is no question, though, they they differ from the generation before. One factor at play here is the growing homogeneity we mentioned earlier.

In today's political spectrum there is less difference between Republicans and Democrats than there was 20 years ago. Is there any difference between a liberal Republican and a conservative Democrat? Not much. Both are firmly establishment, and there is little popular movement for third-party politics. There also is good motivation for the bulk of our population being satisfied with the status quo. Considering the past 30 years, these have been pretty peaceful times for the United States. That is probably the biggest single reason accounting for George Bush's election to the presidency. Voters wanted more of the same. Mr. Bush was the first president since John F. Kennedy to take office without some kind of major crisis looming over this country. Lyndon Johnson assumed the job after the nation was stunned by the assassination of President Kennedy; Richard Nixon came into office during the turbulent 1960s, when the nation was being torn by the Vietnam War; Gerald Ford was thrust into the position when the Watergate scandal forced Mr. Nixon to resign; Jimmy Carter was voted into office after the OPEC oil crisis helped escalate inflation to record heights; and Ronald Reagan was tapped for the post as inflation increased and the country feared for Americans taken hostage in Iran. Looking back on those years, you can see that the problems caused voters to switch back and forth from Democrat to Republican.

When George Bush ran for office in 1988, the only significant national problem was the federal budget deficit; but it was nowhere near as important or emotional an issue as others that confronted presidential candidates over the previous 30 years. If Mr. Bush can steer the country away from war, major scandal, soaring inflation and debilitating recession, American voters will keep him in office until 1996. There will, of course, be many different voters in 1996 than there were in 1988. If you want to see how some of them classify themselves in the political spectrum, we will point out a tracking study conducted by the American Council on Education and the University of California at Los Angeles. Incoming freshmen across the country were asked to identify their political inclinations. In 1988, 24.3% said they viewed themselves as "liberal" or "far left." This was down from a peak of 38.1% reached in 1971, but up a few points from the 1980 low of 21.8%. Among the 1988 freshmen, 21.7% identified themselves as "conservative" or "far right," up from a low of 14.5% in 1973. The biggest single category, however, were those who classified themselves as "middle of the road." They accounted for 53.9%, but down from the peak of 60.3% in 1983.

Before racing to conclusions it should be noted that this survey represents college students only. It doesn't measure the political beliefs of those young people who aren't going on to college. We also must remember these young people are Baby Busters, a much smaller and less influential group than the Baby Boomers.

Embracing Neotraditionalism

Many social observers believe that traditionalism is going to stage a dramatic comeback in the 1990s because of the conservatism of the Baby Boomers. We have already discussed the fine points of the political trends, which are interrelated with the social trends. But what is traditional to a 35-year-old Boomer isn't necessarily traditional to a 65-year-old retiree.

The Boomers have invented their own brand of neotraditionalism, which in part echoes some of their blend of political philosophy. To a Boomer a nuclear family, with Dad at work, Mom at home and two kids in school, is not traditional; it is simply old-fashioned and out of date. You might as well expect a young family to buy a black-and-white console television and put it in their living room.

It is true that there will be a return of interest in family formation and family values in the 1990s. That is because so many Boomers will be in their family-forming years. They have already created a population bubble of youngsters who are moving into elementary schools. As a result, these young families will be more interested in education. They will want to devote more time to their families, seek out wholesome family activities and start saving earlier than any other generation for their children's college education.

But their neotraditionalism includes some provisos that were not part of the old traditionalism:

- When they talk about forming families, a huge percentage of Boomers are really considering having only one child. Nobody ever said that you had to have a large family to enjoy family life. For many Boomers, the family will include *no* children.
- The mother will not stop working permanently when she has a child. Most likely she will take a leave of absence for an average of four months, then return to her old job or a similar one.
- The husband/father will tend to do more of the household chores that previously were considered "woman's work." Women, however, will continue to carry the load of household duties, even if they work full-time outside the home. (After all, we can carry this neotraditionalism *too* far.)
- Boomers will be far more likely than any previous generation to get a divorce if the marriage isn't working out. A woman who has been employed through motherhood will feel more independent. Having fewer children will also make the separation easier.
- Individual members of Boomer families also will have more of their own activities and interests, which do not include other family members. This is another result of two-earner families, where job duties will make their schedules less flexible.

Evaluating Our Values

Such profound concepts as a society's values do not change substantially in only a decade. It takes at least a generation—usually longer—for such changes to be felt. While we can't conduct group psychology on every aspect of American morals and values, there are a few specific areas that deserve attention.

One of them is religion, which is not faring well in modern America. About 68% of Americans say they are members of a church or a synagogue, down from 73% 30 years ago. The percentage of those saying that they attended a religious service in the past week has declined from 47% to 40%. This doesn't mean Americans are turning anti-God. What they are doing is turning a deaf ear toward organized religions. Studies show that more than 95% of Americans believe in God, but about one-third feel that organized religions are too restrictive. Despite this, the 1980s produced an increase in the number of Americans participating in fundamentalist sects. This may be running counter to the overall trend because so many fundamentalist clergymen established "television ministries." They apparently produced the right product for the times, allowing Americans to witness religious services from the convenience of their own living rooms. A cloud has been cast over the future of fundamentalist religions because of the scandals associated with Jimmy Swaggart, Jim and Tammy Faye Bakker, and other television preachers. Publicity surrounding the allegations of impropriety and personal use of church funds may well discourage newcomers from experimenting with fundamentalism.

We would guess (projections are impossible) that the number of people claiming membership in fundamentalist religions will be in direct proportion to the number of hours such services are broadcast on television. In contemporary America even religion must be marketed to the consumers.

In terms of all religions, it is very difficult to project any well-defined trends because of so many conflicting indicators. On the positive side, our aging population bodes well for religions. The older people are, the more likely they are to be members of a church or synagogue. Of those over 50, 75% are members. The fact that so many Boomers will be forming families in the next decade also is a positive sign. Family members are more likely to be churchgoers than single persons.

On the other hand, geography is important to religious practice. Among people who live in the western states, only 57% are church members, about 15 percentage points lower than the other three sections of the country. As we pointed out earlier, the West is the fastest-growing region of the country.

Research also shows that the poor and less educated are more likely to practice a religion than those in upper demographic categories. Trends toward a higher educational level and an increase in the upper income categories may well signal a decline in religious participation.

The rapid influx of Hispanics into the United States will cause the number of Roman Catholics to increase through the 1990s, although church going will continue to lag. The Catholic church has been facing another major problem for years, a steep decline in the number of men going into the priesthood. Some of the church's doctrine, particularly the ban on birth control, celibacy for priests and prohibition of women from priesthood, will not sit well with twenty-first century Americans.

Asian immigration will increase the practice of Buddhism and other Eastern religions in the United States. We also expect that some Americans who dislike the organizational aspects of religion will switch to more individual means of worship, such as meditation, family prayer and various forms of volunteerism.

Our projection is that religious participation will remain stable through the rest of this century, but then will increase in the first decade of the twenty-first century as the Baby Boomers start approaching senior citizen status. There is something about reaching an advanced age that makes people start thinking more about religion. Perhaps the reason can be found in a reader survey conducted by *Better Homes and Gardens* on the subject of religion and spirituality. The magazine found that 89% of its readers believe in eternal life, 87% believe in heaven, and 76% believe in hell.

Sex, Booze and All Those Good Things

Aside from practicing religion, other values in American culture are changing slowly, if at all. Attitudes toward sex have turned more conservative in the late 1980s, but that is due more to the fear of AIDS and other sexually transmitted diseases than a return to the innocence of the 1950s and before. We could, of course, write volumes about AIDS and the impact that it will have on both heterosexuals and homosexuals in the coming years. As long as there is no prospect for a cure or preventive vaccine, the syndrome will continue to exert a chilling effect on the sexual behavior of concerned Americans.

The sexual revolution of the 1960s occurred in large part because so many young people tested the authority of the older generation. As the number of adolescents and young adults declines in the 1990s, we would expect the older generation to regain some of the influence it lost in the past few decades. This will be considered not so much a backlash as a moderation or compromise among differing views on sexual freedom. This doesn't mean that we will return to Victorian mores. More likely it indicates that sexual freedom and explicitness in the next ten years will not be extended beyond where it is now. We even see a decline in the pornography industry. The aging of the population will be at the crux of this moderating trend. The trend will increase gradually over the next decade, then be reinforced during the following decade as the number of senior citizens increases dramatically. Other "vices" such as smoking and alcohol consumption will also be influenced toward moderation. Smoking will not be eliminated from our society by 2000, but it will be limited to a tiny fraction of the population. The moderating effects of an older population combined with the increased health consciousness of Americans will also change the nature of drinking. Rather than the routine cocktail before lunch and wine with dinner, drinking will be reserved for special occasions. (Perhaps it's time for someone to invent a cocktail that contains prune juice.)

One last aspect of values that should get some attention is the American attitude toward charitable giving. In that regard, our society has gradually increased its generosity over the past few decades. From $16.2 billion in 1970, the amount of money individuals contributed to charitable organizations more than doubled to $40.7 billion in 1980 and was expected to double again to more than $80 billion by 1990. While individual giving continued on the upswing, contributions by corporations stopped growing in the late 1980s. Without a change in tax laws, corporate giving probably will continue to lag in the next decade. What most people do not realize, however, is that corporations account for only about 5% of charitable giving, while individuals account for more than 80%. The rest comes from foundations and bequests. Just as with fundamentalist religions, we presume that charitable corporations have collected more funds because they have marketed themselves more adroitly in the 1980s than they did in previous decades. The other significant factor is that religions are the biggest single category of charities, accounting for nearly half of the contributions.

One last interesting point about contributions is that the lowest income group of Americans, those with annual incomes under $10,000, give the highest percentage of their incomes, about 3%, to charity. Only those in the over-$50,000 bracket come close to the same level of giving. While the growth in two-income families will tend to push up individual giving in the 1990s, it will have a depressing effect on volunteerism. Mothers who have full-time jobs as well as families to care for, simply will not have the time to devote to volunteer work. The only real opportunity for an increase in volunteerism in the coming years will be if those over 65 can be induced into such work. Statistics show, however, that of all age cohorts over the age of 14, those 65 and over have the lowest level of volunteer participation. The volunteer situation could even become critical in the first decade of the twenty-first century when the number of over-65s shoots up rapidly.

Our Attitude Toward Work

Although we covered work prospects and careers in another chapter, we thought this would be the most appropriate spot to discuss the changing work ethic in this country. It probably has more to do with values than with what kind of jobs will open up in the future. Our basic contention is that two-way loyalty between employee and employer is on the wane. This, first of all, presumes that such loyalty ever existed. There is no way to prove or disprove it, so we can only comment on our observations. One such observation, and perhaps the most important aspect in the erosion of loyalty, is that employee longevity has been devalued. Many major American corporations, former models of management excellence like AT&T and Sears, Roebuck, had based their successful performance for decades on the loyalty of long-time employees.

Countless blue chip companies welcomed young employees right out of school, sent them to training programs and gradually moved them up the corporate ladder until they were top managers. Even if the employee did not have management potential, their longevity was valued. They received bonuses for years on the job and were given company stock and allowed to buy more at a discount. After 40 years, such employees were given a gold watch and a going-away party; then they retired to live off a nice pension.

Somewhere in the mid-1970s this was no longer considered a smart management technique. Short-term profits became more important than long-term growth. Workers were fired when their productivity lagged, or they were forced to take early retirement with reduced benefits. The conglomerating and downsizing trend of the 1980s was a signal to employees that no one could be secure in his or her job. Dozens of major American corporations were taken over by acquisition – some hostile, some amicable. Hundreds of thousands of workers who thought they had jobs for life were suddenly fired or laid off for the good of the bottom line. This phenomenon became so prevalent in the late 1970s and early 1980s that it led to the development of a new consulting specialty called outplacement. Outplacement firms were hired by corporations to help dismissed employees find jobs elsewhere. Usually these services were reserved for top and middle management, but when corporations engaged in wholesale firings, they set up in-house outplacement operations to help all employees organize a job search.

Many top managers were kissed goodbye by their companies with lavish severance packages that paid their salary for months or even years and sometimes provided them with enough largesse to live out the rest of their years without having to worry about further employment. While this was happening, the new employees coming into corporations were not as interested in longevity. Their aim was to get as high a starting salary as possible, and within two years of getting the job they would start looking elsewhere for a better spot. This tendency has been documented by research in the mid-1980s that showed that a majority of recent college graduates worked for more than one employer within 18 months of graduation. In addition, only 13% of them said they expected to stay with their current employer for as long as five years. Corporations were faced with a new problem, called "salary compression," where entry-level people coming out of college were receiving higher pay than other employees who had been doing the same job for several years. Because they needed to increase their work forces, the companies paid the high starting salaries.

The combination of these factors, along with the continuing trend of mergers and acquisitions, contributed heavily to the decline in loyalty. Two Clemson University professors have even suggested that employees are more likely to engage in sabotage when their companies are merged or acquired. They feel helpless about the changes taking place without any input from them.

It is virtually impossible to project whether this trend will continue through the next decade. It depends to some extent on whether merger activity continues. It also depends on what managements do to alter the attitudes of their workers and engender loyalty from them. Of course if the managers don't feel any great sense of loyalty, how can they be expected to elicit any from their workers?

Another related concept we should mention is that of the American work ethic, if there is such a thing. There seems to be a consensus, but very little proof, by observers that the work ethic is declining in the United States. Some say that tardiness and absenteeism are increasing while diligence and care are decreasing. We can approach this concept only philosophically. If the work ethic is different today from what it was 50 or 100 years ago, it is because the people are different. When the flood of European immigrants came to this country they worked for survival. Money was important to them because it bought them food and shelter, and perhaps a college education for their children. Money is still important to workers today, but maybe it is not needed as desperately as it was during the heyday of the Industrial Revolution. This will be a challenge to employers in the coming years because many of them have used only money or money equivalents as an inducement to workers. These are not the motivating factors they used to be. Increasingly workers say they are looking for more job satisfaction; and it appears that many of them are getting it. In the late 1980s the Wyatt Company conducted an extensive study of 5,000 workers across the country and found that 48% of them were generally satisfied with their pay levels, and 58% were satisfied with their employee benefits. More than two-thirds of the workers felt their jobs were interesting, but only 35% felt their companies offered good opportunities for advancement. This uncertainty about the future seemed to undermine their commitment to the company. Only 39% said they looked at their company as "more than just a place to work."

If we can assume that employee loyalty is desirable and important, then we can deduce that managers will have a great challenge in the 1990s. They will have to reignite the fires of employee loyalty and reestablish a two-way commitment with their workers. Because of this, we predict there will be a great demand for employee motivation services and consulting in the 1990s. These worker attitudes, when coupled with the oncoming labor shortage, will force employers to address the problem of low morale. This is already under way with the adoption of some Japanese management tactics. It also might mean a complete flip-flop in management priorities. The Japanese have long felt that the work force is the companies' number one priority, followed by the customers and lastly by the stockholders. In the United States, our priorities are reversed. Is one way right and the other wrong? Only the next decade will tell.

ADVISORY

Trends

- Americans are assimilating into one society, but at a painstakingly slow rate.
- Increased travel and global communications will draw the residents of industrialized countries closer together, making them more alike.
- More Americans will become political centrists, with fewer on the fringes of right and left. They prefer the status quo, however, because we have escaped the dissension, unrest and violence of the 1960s.
- Baby Boomers, entering their peak family-forming years, will start a new brand of traditionalism derived from their attitudes and lifestyles.
- Participation in organized religions is declining but may rise when the Boomers hit retirement age. Americans seem to be more conservative about sex and are shunning vices like smoking and drinking.
- The work ethic is changing, with a decline in employer-employee loyalty. Leisure time and benefits have become more important to workers.

Strategies

- As residents of different countries become more alike, more kinds of products will have export potential.
- Corporate image builders should shun radical political/social positions and develop middle-American positions, which is where most of the populace is.
- Religions should segment just as marketers do. An intellectual orientation should appeal to the growing ranks of highly educated.
- Faced with a labor shortage in the 1990s, employers may have to shift their work rules and policies to adapt to the new work ethic.

INDEX